I0560501

VOICES

STEPPING OUT OF THE DARKNESS AND INTO THE LIGHT

A JOURNEY OF SPIRITUAL
AWAKENING, HEALING, AND
INNER TRANSFORMATION

CHERYL T CAMPBELL

ISBN: 978-1-968061-19-7

To Alan, my partner, my friend, and my greatest teacher. Your steadfast love and quiet strength have been my foundation, and the lessons you've taught me—often unexpected—have shaped me in ways I never imagined. You are the anchor of my soul and the light that illuminates my path.

To Ian, the son of my heart. I am so grateful for the day you came into my life. Your presence is a blessing I never saw coming, and one I will cherish always.

To my parents, Helen and Leo Tancreti, for your unwavering support and for instilling in me the entrepreneurial spirit that continues to guide my journey.

Table of Contents

Awakening the Soul

"This journey asks something bold of you—to step outside your comfort zone and into the unknown. Growth begins where certainty ends, and in the space between, you'll find the truth of who you are. Take what resonates, and leave the rest, but stay curious. What you set aside today may hold the key to your tomorrow."

A Question That Sparks the Journey

"The journey of awakening begins not with answers but with the courage to ask the questions that stir your soul."

A Question That Lingers

"Why the hell are we here?" Lisa's voice cut through the steady rhythm of the waves, a question that didn't just float in the air but lingered—settling deep in my chest. It wasn't the first time I'd thought about it, but hearing it aloud made it feel heavier, more urgent. It stopped me in my tracks—not just because of its bluntness, but because it was so raw, so undeniably real. It was a question you couldn't ignore, one that demanded to be felt as much as answered.

Earlier that morning, I'd made my way down to the beach to meet Lisa for coffee. The air had that crisp edge of autumn, carrying the scent of salt and the promise of rain. Waves rolled in with their familiar rhythm, a comforting sound I'd grown up with, a reminder that some things never change. Above us, seagulls danced effortlessly in the wind, oblivious to the brewing storm. The world felt alive, even in its wildness.

Lisa and I hadn't seen each other in months. Life had swept us in different directions, as it often did. But that morning, sitting on the sand with our coffee, it felt like no time had passed. We dove into our usual catch-up routine—the kind of conversation that skips small talk and goes straight for the heart. I told her about my dad's latest battle with cancer and how he'd survived but lost his eye in the process. She shared the joy of her new grandchild, a bright light in what she admitted had been a challenging year. And then, with a thoughtful pause, she dropped the question.

"What's it all about? Why the hell are we here?"

The Courage to Ask

The weight of her words settled over us, blending with the sound of the waves. It wasn't just Lisa's question; it was everyone's question. It was my question. And it was likely yours, too. There we were, two friends on a beach, trying to make sense of the world and our place in it. The simplicity of the moment was disarming, the kind of quiet clarity that sneaks up on you when you're least expecting it.

I took a deep breath, letting the salty air fill my lungs. "I think we're here for a reason," I said, more to myself than to her. "I think, deep down, we all know it too. We just forget."

Lisa tilted her head, her eyes searching mine. "Forget what?"

"That our souls chose this," I replied. "This life, this moment in time—it's not random. I don't think there are coincidences anymore. I think we're here with a purpose, even if we can't always see it."

The words felt both terrifying and comforting to say aloud. Terrifying because admitting it meant believing it. Comforting because it meant there was more to the story than the chaos we often see on the surface.

Lisa nodded slowly, her gaze drifting to the horizon. "So, you're saying we're all connected? That this is part of something bigger?"

"Exactly."

At that moment, it felt like the universe had paused, as if nodding in agreement. The wind swirled around us, the waves continued their dance with the shore, and I felt a quiet certainty settle in my heart. This wasn't just a conversation; it was a reminder—a nudge to remember the truth we so often forget in the busyness of life.

A Call to Remember

That question didn't just linger—it became a quiet guide, like a whisper from my soul, showing up in moments of uncertainty and reminding me of the unfolding path of my own awakening. It wasn't an invitation to begin but a call to continue—a deeper exploration of the growth and healing that had already shaped my journey.

As Lisa and I sat on that beach, I didn't have all the answers. I still don't. But what I do have is a deep understanding that we're all on a path of awakening. If you're reading this, I believe it's not by chance. Some part of you already knows there's more—and you're ready to remember.

So, let's dive in together. I'll share my stories, challenges, and triumphs— not because I have it all figured out, but because I hope my journey will shed some light on yours. We're all stepping out of the darkness and into the light, one question, one experience, one day at a time. Awakening isn't a destination. It's an unfolding—a remembering of who you truly are beneath the noise, the roles, and the expectations. It often begins with a soft nudge or an inner knowing that life is asking something more of you. That call might be quiet at first, but once heard, it's hard to ignore.

Answering the Whisper

That spark—the one that stirs something deep within—often begins with a single question. But the answers we seek aren't always found in books or lectures. More often, they arrive through lived experience, whispered to us through the world around us.

In *Part 1—Beginnings and Belonging*, we return to the foundation of connection—how we relate to the natural world, to those we love, and, ultimately, to ourselves. These connections ground us, offering insights and lessons that guide us as we awaken to the truth of who we are.

The first chapter in this section takes us into the wild, where an encounter with a coyote taught me about the sacred threads that bind us all. Through its quiet wisdom, I began to see how nature offers profound answers to the questions of the soul. Let's step into this story.

PART 1
Beginnings and Belonging

"True belonging begins not with the world around us but within. To find your place in the universe, you must first step into the wilderness of your own soul and claim who you are."

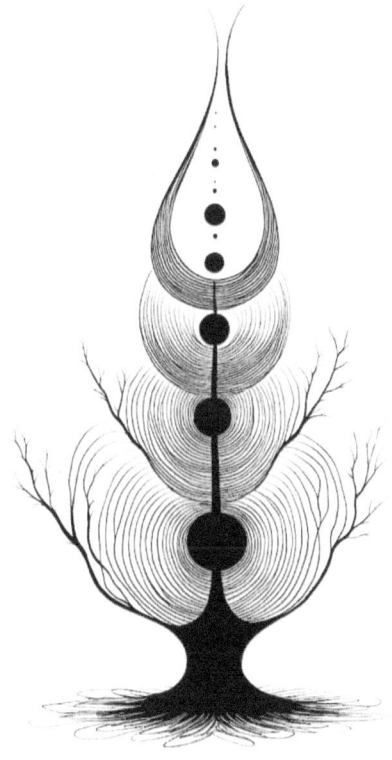

Lessons from the Wild—
A Coyote's Wisdom

"In the quiet of the wild, we find reflections of ourselves—
reminders of our connection to all that is."

Some moments in life remind us of the deep, often mysterious connection we share with the natural world. I recently experienced one of those moments in a way that left me both awed and reflective.

It was a quiet morning, and I was sitting outdoors meditating. The air was crisp, and the early morning sounds surrounded me—birds singing, leaves rustling, the gentle hum of nature waking up. I was lost in the thought that we are all one—deeply connected to everything around us.

When I opened my eyes, there he was—just fifteen feet away—a coyote sitting in complete stillness, watching me with a calm, penetrating gaze. Time seemed to pause as our eyes locked. It wasn't fear I felt, but a profound connection—a recognition, as though this wild creature and I shared some unspoken understanding. The moment stretched out endlessly—then vanished in a heartbeat. As quietly as he had appeared, the coyote turned and slipped back across the field, disappearing into the woods.

I sat there breathless replaying the moment in my mind. What had just happened? Why had this creature appeared to me during a moment of stillness? The encounter felt sacred—as if the universe had whispered a secret just for me.

The Coyote as a Symbol

Animals are seen as messengers or guides in many cultures and spiritual traditions, bringing symbolic meanings and insights. The coyote, in particular, is a fascinating figure—often associated with transformation, adaptability, and playfulness. Thriving in diverse environments, the coyote embodies resilience.

Coyotes are also known for their trickster energy—able to navigate life's challenges with a sense of humor and cleverness. In some Native American traditions, the coyote is seen as a teacher, delivering lessons that often arrive through unexpected or unconventional means. When a coyote crosses your path, it may be a sign that life is inviting you to embrace change, trust your instincts, and perhaps not take things too seriously.

For those who are new to exploring symbolism in nature, this idea might feel unfamiliar—or even far-fetched. But think about the moments when a song, a stranger's words, or an animal's appearance felt perfectly timed—as though life was responding to your inner world. Nature often speaks in whispers, using signs and symbols to guide us toward deeper truths.

The coyote is one such symbol. It reminds us to stay curious and open to life's subtle lessons.

A Sacred Moment of Connection

Encountering a coyote during meditation felt deeply significant to me. Meditation is a practice that connects me with my inner self and the world around me. In that moment of stillness, I felt more attuned to the subtle energies of the environment—open to experiences that might otherwise go unnoticed.

The coyote's appearance felt like a powerful affirmation of the oneness I was contemplating. It was as if the universe itself had acknowledged my thoughts—sending this wild creature as a reminder that I am, indeed, part of the great web of life.

When our eyes met, it wasn't just an exchange of glances. It was a conversation without words—a moment of mutual recognition between two beings who, for an instant, were completely present with each other.

What Did the Coyote Teach Me?

The encounter left me with three powerful reminders—each one offering a different kind of wisdom.

First, it reminded me to stay adaptable. Life is full of unexpected twists and turns, and like the coyote, I can navigate these changes with resilience and flexibility. His presence urged me to trust in my ability to handle whatever comes my way—and to embrace change rather than resist it.

Second, there's the lesson of mindfulness. The coyote appeared when I was fully present during meditation, reminding me of the importance of staying grounded and aware, even in everyday life. It's in those quiet, mindful moments that I often receive the most profound insights or messages from the universe.

Lastly, the coyote reminded me not to take life too seriously. Even in the midst of challenges, there's always room for a bit of playfulness and humor. This doesn't mean ignoring the weight of life's difficulties, but approaching them with a light heart—knowing that everything is part of the natural ebb and flow.

From the Wild to the Heart

Whether I view the coyote as a spiritual guide, a messenger, or simply a fellow creature sharing the earth with me, this encounter holds deep meaning. It reminds me that I am never truly alone—that there's a vast, interconnected world of beings, seen and unseen, all around me.

The coyote's visit during my meditation was an invitation to explore the qualities of adaptability, resilience, and playfulness in my own life.

Reflecting on this experience, I'm reminded of the book's overarching theme—stepping out of the darkness and into the light. Each connection, each encounter, is a step forward, reminding us of the beauty, the lessons, and the light that is always within reach.

The wild teaches us about the interwoven nature of life. But it's often in the quiet moments with our closest companions—our pets—that we discover the purest expressions of love.

If nature is the classroom, then the animals we share our lives with are the most devoted teachers—showing us how to live with open hearts. Through their unwavering loyalty and unspoken wisdom, they reflect the best parts of ourselves.

They remind us that the lessons of love aren't found in grand gestures, but in everyday moments of connection—always waiting to be embraced.

As we journey further, we'll uncover the depth of love and wisdom our closest companions quietly share, offering profound lessons for the heart and soul.

Guardians of the Soul—Awakening Through Our Dogs' Love

"In their silent wisdom, our pets teach us lessons about love, loyalty, and the courage to live fully in the present."

The bonds that shape us are rarely loud. They come quietly, with wet noses and wagging tails, offering love that speaks directly to the soul.

Dogs have always held a special place in my heart. Their unconditional love, loyalty, and wisdom are gifts I've cherished deeply. Over the years, I've been blessed to share my life with several incredible dogs, each leaving an indelible mark on my soul. But it was Blu, Milly, Peach, Andy, and Savannah who taught me lessons I never expected—lessons that reached into the deepest parts of my being and reminded me of the resilience, joy, and capacity for love we all carry within us.

Each of them came into my life at a unique moment, as if guided by divine timing. Through their presence, I began to understand the profound connection between humans and animals—one that transcends words and touches the soul. These dogs didn't just change my life. They awakened parts of me I didn't know needed healing.

Blu—The Katrina Survivor

We weren't in any hurry to bring a dog into our home. My stepson—the son of my heart—had a deep fear of dogs, and we wanted to wait until he was ready to embrace the experience. When the time finally came, we looked to a rescue group, and that's when Blu came into our lives.

We suspected he was a Katrina dog—one of the many animals displaced by the devastating hurricane. The rescue group had us sign special papers agreeing that if his family ever came forward within a year, we would have to return him. Thankfully, that day never came. Blu was part of our family now—and he was incredible.

Blu had a way of filling our home with his gentle presence. Despite suffering from separation anxiety, he quickly became a beloved member of our family. His quirks—like how he would get into anything and everything that reminded him of us when we left the house—only endeared him to us more. His need to be close to us was a reminder of the trauma he had likely endured before finding his way to our home.

Through Blu, I learned that love has the power to transform even the most wounded hearts. He reminded me that our scars, while painful, don't define us—they're proof of our survival. Blu's resilience became my inspiration, showing me that second chances are not only possible but also beautiful.

Milly's Arrival—A Healing Presence

Our journey with Blu led to a deeper involvement with the rescue group. We decided to become a foster family, eager to help more dogs find their forever homes. But we weren't very good at fostering—we were too quick to fall in love.

Within the first week of fostering, we adopted Milly, a sweet soul who fit perfectly into our growing family.

Milly's story was one of survival and resilience. Found on the streets in the South, she had been so beaten down and fearful that she needed to be placed with a special foster family to help socialize her. When she came to us, she was fiercely independent. She only allowed us to pet her on her backside—and only when she wanted.

Despite this, she became our protector. She would patrol our property in wide circles, creating a path still visible months after her passing.

It took almost a year before she trusted us enough to give her a belly rub. Watching her journey from fear to trust was a revelation. Milly showed me that healing isn't linear—it's a process built on patience, love, and the willingness to show up, even when it's hard.

Her story mirrored my own journey of opening my heart to vulnerability. She taught me that while independence is a strength, true connection requires trust.

Peach—The Unexpected Addition

Not long after, Peach came into our lives. She was supposed to be a temporary guest, brought up from the South for a meet-and-greet with a family interested in adopting her. But when they decided she wasn't the right fit, it became clear that Peach was meant to stay with us.

Despite the rescue group's insistence that we post her profile on Petfinder, I couldn't bear the thought of letting her go. My husband felt the same way. Peach was ours to care for—and she brought a joy into our home that was completely her own.

Peach had been through unimaginable abuse, but her spirit was unbroken. She greeted each day with an enthusiasm that was contagious. Every step she took without chains, every butterfly she chased, and every new path she explored was a testament to her unshakable optimism.

And then there was her dance. Every time Peach headed down the stairs for a walk or a meal, she would break into what we lovingly called **"the Peachy Pie Wiggle."** Her backside would sway and hop in pure, wiggly delight—an exuberant little celebration of life's simplest pleasures. Watching her move like that, tail high and hips dancing, was enough to make anyone smile.

Peach taught me that joy is a choice—a decision to see beauty even in the midst of life's challenges. She reminded me that healing doesn't erase the past, but it can transform it into something that brings gratitude.

From Peach, I learned to savor the small, everyday moments—to embrace the present as a gift.

Andy—The Unexpected Blessing

Just when we thought our family was complete, Andy found his way to us—ten months after Peach. His arrival was truly unexpected. My chiropractor had purchased Andy on a whim but quickly realized he wasn't cut out to be a dog "owner."

The first time I saw Andy, he was in a crate—and I instantly fell in love with him. He was unusually lethargic for a puppy, and I suspect it was because he spent about 18 hours a day in that crate. I won't delve too deeply into my thoughts on that, but regardless of how he was treated in his first year, it happened so he could find his way home to us.

The day I learned that Doc was going to rehome Andy, I left the office, burst into tears, and called my husband, crying, "He's getting rid of Andy!" With three large dogs already occupying our apartment, Al shocked me with his next comment: "We'll take him."

When I picked up Andy a few days later, I brought him to the job site where Al was working, as they had never met before. Something strange and wonderful happened. This lethargic pup grew more and more excited as we approached the site. The closer we got, the greater his excitement. As the car came to a stop, Andy scrambled over the seat and practically jumped out of the window and into Al's arms. It was as if he already knew—he was finally home.

Over our fifteen years together, Andy has taught me so many lessons that it's difficult to name just a few. Still, his love showed me how to be more compassionate and understanding—to be there for others quietly in the background. He taught me that comfort comes in many different forms.

Andy's quiet strength and unwavering loyalty reminded me that sometimes, the most profound impact comes from simply being present and offering love without expectation. His bond with Al became a testament to the power of knowing where you belong—a feeling we all long for and cherish when it's found.

That moment when Andy instinctively wanted to jump into Al's arms has stayed with me. It felt like a profound reminder that we all carry within us the ability to recognize "home"—not as a physical place, but as a connection to love, belonging, and safety.

Andy also taught me the importance of quiet presence. He didn't seek attention or make a fuss, but his love was steady and unwavering. In a world where so much is loud and demanding, Andy reminded me that the most meaningful acts of love often come in silence. Simply being there for someone—without expectation, without fanfare—can be the greatest gift of all.

Savanah—The Wise Elder

Savannah, the last to join our family, arrived a year after the passing of Blu and Peach. She was a chocolate lab, already ten years old when she became part of our lives. Though our time together was short—only three years—her impact was profound.

Savannah suffered from severe allergies, scratching herself raw. But after we adjusted her diet and introduced a new allergy medication, she transformed. It was as if she became a puppy again—frolicking in the fields and embracing a newfound zest for life.

Savannah taught me that you are never too old to experience something new—to rediscover joy regardless of your age. Watching her go from a dog burdened by discomfort to one dancing through fields was nothing short of magical. She reminded me, and perhaps even reminded herself, that life's beauty isn't measured in years but in our openness to the moment.

Her gentle wisdom and playful spirit taught me that renewal is always possible—no matter where we are in our journey.

The Heartbreak of Loss

Loss is inevitable when you open your heart—but the lessons love teaches are worth the pain. Each of my dogs has left an imprint on my soul, but Blu and Peach reminded me that even in loss, love endures.

In 2012, I found myself in Las Vegas, speaking at an event near Lake Nevada. It was a professional milestone, but my heart was far from the stage. Barely twelve hours into my trip, I received a call from my husband. Blu was so distressed that he had been rushed to our vet, who then referred him to an emergency clinic thirty minutes away.

My husband didn't have the heart to deal with the vet directly, so I immediately took over communication with the staff at Piper Memorial.

The next forty-eight hours were a blur of anxiety and helplessness. Every time I prepared to take the stage or participate in a roundtable, I was faced with another decision about Blu's treatment. The staff at Piper Memorial was incredible—compassionate, dedicated, and genuinely caring. I was especially touched when I called one morning and the vet who had been caring for Blu answered the phone on her day off. He had touched her heart so deeply that she came in just to see how he was doing.

Saturday night brought a glimmer of hope. The staff called to say Blu had gotten up, walked outside, and relieved himself for the first time in days. The sense of relief I felt was overwhelming. I allowed myself to enjoy dinner with my fellow speakers that evening believing Blu was finally on the mend.

But my relief was short-lived.

In the early morning hours—just before I was set to leave for the airport—the phone rang again. Blu had taken a turn for the worse. The vet explained that, while he had fought hard, the odds of his survival were now painfully low. As much as she admired his spirit, she gently told me it was time to let him go.

My heart shattered. Not just for the loss of Blu, but for the knowledge that my husband had to face that moment alone—and that Blu didn't have either of us by his side when he passed.

The pain was unbearable. And then... we received a sympathy card from the clinic, signed by all seven staff members who had cared for Blu. Each note expressed how special he was—and that he was not alone.

Even though I had been more than 2,600 miles away, there was a strange comfort in knowing he had been surrounded by love when he left this earth.

Peach's Final Days— A Miraculous Message

Four weeks after Blu passed, I found myself in Utah for a three-day business retreat. I was staying at the breathtaking Timber Moose Lodge—the largest private log cabin in the United States. This majestic property, with over 26,000 square feet of living space, sat on twelve private acres in the Utah mountains, offering commanding 360° views from its 9,000 square feet of outdoor decks and balconies.

Despite the stunning surroundings, my heart sank on the very first evening when I received a call from Al. Peach had lost the ability to walk.

I felt an overwhelming dread—how could I face this again, so soon after losing Blu? My gut told me it was her time, but I also knew I needed to be with her. Yet I was miles away, with no easy way home. Did I have the right to ask her to wait for me?

Then something miraculous happened.

A young woman I had just met that morning, Kelly, approached me. Hesitantly, she said, "I know you'll think I'm crazy, but I received a message meant for you. A dog came to me in my dreams. I could tell she was scared, but I also sensed she was patiently waiting for you. I hope this has meaning for you?"

Her words struck me like lightning—and I nearly burst into tears. Peach had reached out to me through this stranger, letting me know she understood and would wait for me.

Knowing Peach could no longer climb the stairs to our living space, Al slept by her side on the workshop floor, comforting her through the night.

When I returned, we gathered under Peach's favorite tree, with Andy and Milly by our side, waiting for our vet to arrive. Our sweet Peach had endured seven hard years of abuse before she found her way to us, but we were blessed with six wonderful years together. It was a privilege to be by her side when she passed—surrounded by the love and comfort she had come to know as her family.

The Dream—A Wake-Up Call

Four months after their passing—and long after Peach's miraculous message through Kelly—I had another visitation. This time, in a dream,

Blu appeared with Peach by his side. He didn't say much—just a simple command: "Snap out of it and look inside." I didn't fully understand the meaning, but the dream stayed with me, nagging at the edges of my consciousness.

In the weeks that followed, I began to realize that the profound sadness I had been carrying since their deaths wasn't just grief—it was something deeper. I had slipped into depression, something I was reluctant to admit, even to myself.

The more I reflected, the more I recognized that this depression wasn't solely about losing Blu and Peach. It was tied to a much darker period in my life—a time when I had lost eight friends in one year and had buried the pain so deeply that I hadn't even allowed myself to grieve.

Their message was clear: I needed to face the emotions I had hidden away for so long. Slowly, I began to process my grief—not just for them, but for all the losses I had endured. As I did, I felt myself coming back to life, integrating the emotions that had been locked away in the darkness and bringing them into the light.

Coming Full Circle

I am grateful for the lessons Blu, Milly, Peach, Andy, and Savannah taught me. They reminded me of the importance of confronting our emotions—of not burying our pain so deeply that it becomes a silent weight on our hearts. Through their love, their lives, and even their deaths, they helped me find my way back to myself.

Reflecting on that time, I realized these lessons were just the beginning. The emotions they unlocked led me to confront immense grief and embrace healing. Blu, Milly, Peach, and Savannah may be gone, but their spirits live on in the lessons they left behind—and for that, I will always be grateful.

As I write this, I find myself coming to terms with the reality that Andy's time with us is drawing to a close. The vet has given us the heartbreaking news that he has only a few months left. We've moved our bedroom to the lower level of the barn, where Andy can be close to us, as the stairs have become too much for him.

We treasure each moment we have with him, knowing that—like the others—his spirit will remain a guiding presence in our lives long after he's gone.

Preparing the Way

The love and connection we share with animals teach us so much about who we are. But these lessons often serve as stepping stones to something greater—they are bridges to understanding our own souls.

These faithful companions remind us of the courage it takes to heal, the joy of living authentically, and the resilience found in unconditional love. Yet their greatest gift lies in what they awaken within us—the ability to see ourselves more clearly.

Through their silent wisdom, they don't just comfort us—they prepare us.

For the turning inward.

For the unraveling of who we thought we were.

For the path of remembering who we truly are.

As we take the next steps on this journey, we'll begin to explore the unfolding of spiritual awakening—not as a single moment, but as a series of sacred stages that reveal our highest potential, one layer at a time.

The Five Stages of Awakening—A Path to Higher Self-Discovery

"Spiritual growth is like climbing a mountain—the higher you ascend, the clearer the view of your soul and its connection to the universe."

Before any transformation can occur, there is a stirring—a subtle yet profound realization that life holds more than what we've known. This initial awakening isn't always dramatic; sometimes it's a quiet acknowledgment that our current path no longer aligns with our inner truth. While each journey looks different, there are stages we pass through—waypoints that invite deeper awareness and greater connection to something beyond ourselves. The path of awakening may not be linear, but it is always sacred.

The Awakening

The Awakening is the first stage—where we begin to question the way we see the world and our place in it. It's when we realize that there's more to life than what we've been taught, and that the truth is far more expansive. This often involves reexamining long-held beliefs—passed down by family, culture, or religion—and feeling drawn to explore something deeper.

For me, The Awakening didn't happen in a single moment. It was more like a slow, steady unraveling of the beliefs I had grown up with.

My family wasn't religious, but we went to church, and I was raised with the basic teachings of Catholicism. I have vivid memories of sitting in the wooden pews, surrounded by the smells of incense and the soft murmur of prayers. It was a comforting routine in many ways—but even as a child, I felt an underlying sense of unease.

That unease was hard to articulate back then, but now I recognize it as my soul's quiet voice—gently urging me to question what didn't resonate. Even at that young age, there was a part of me that noticed when love and truth were overshadowed by fear and control. That realization would take years to fully understand, but it planted the seeds for my spiritual journey.

I remember hearing that we were all born in sin—and that we needed redemption from our very first breath. That didn't make sense to me. If God was all-loving, why would He create us with something inherently wrong?

That was one of the first cracks in the foundation: the idea that love and fear could somehow be woven together in the church's teachings.

As I grew older, these questions only deepened. By my early teens, I was struggling to understand why so much seemed to be based on fear—fear of sin, fear of hell, fear of not living up to impossible standards. If God was meant to be loving and forgiving, why was so much of what I had learned rooted in fear?

And then there was the church itself. If its teachings were the "word of God," how could they be changed? How could canon law be rewritten by men, if it was supposed to reflect eternal truth?

This inner conflict created a restlessness I couldn't ignore. It wasn't just about religion—it was about the way the world seemed to operate on rules that didn't align with my inner knowing. My questioning wasn't a rejection of faith; it was a call to find a deeper, truer connection to the divine.

These questions kept rising within me, but I couldn't find the answers in the structured religion I had been raised in. Looking back, I realize that this was the beginning of my spiritual awakening. It was a quiet but persistent shift—a feeling that there was something more to discover. Something beyond the fear, the rules, and the rituals.

I didn't have the language for it at the time, but that inner questioning was the first step toward a broader, more expansive understanding of spirituality.

Have you ever felt the pull to question everything you've been taught? To wonder if the world is far more than the sum of its rules and rituals?

That's The Awakening—a nudge from your soul, inviting you to explore the unknown.

The Seeking

After the initial spark of awakening, The Seeking stage begins. This is when we feel drawn to explore the unknown—searching for answers that help us better understand our spiritual nature. It's a period of curiosity and discovery, often marked by a hunger for knowledge and new experiences. Many of us dive into books, practices, or communities that open our eyes to different perspectives on spirituality—all in the pursuit of deeper understanding.

This phase came for me in my late teens and early twenties. I've always been an avid reader, but during this time, my reading choices shifted toward books that explored the mysteries of the unseen world. I devoured topics like channeling, self-hypnosis, and automatic writing—anything that promised to unlock a deeper connection with the spiritual realm. It felt like I was peeling back the layers of reality, uncovering secrets that had always been there, waiting for me to discover them.

The Seeking stage is often one of trial and error—testing new ideas and practices to see what resonates. At times, it can feel overwhelming, as if the more we learn, the more we realize how much we don't know. But that curiosity is the fuel that keeps us moving forward, even when the path feels unclear.

One of the things that captured my attention was astrology. We had a family friend who practiced it and often did readings for people. I was fascinated by how the movements of planets and stars could supposedly influence our personalities and life paths. It felt like peeking into a cosmic blueprint, and I wanted to know more.

I remember sitting with her, listening intently as she explained how my birth chart revealed aspects of my personality I hadn't fully acknowledged yet. It was another doorway to understanding myself on a deeper level— and I eagerly walked through it.

Around the same time, I visited a psychic for the first time. I wasn't sure what to expect, but I remember being completely astonished by what she told me. She mentioned details about my childhood I had never known—specific events and situations that seemed impossible for a stranger to guess. When I brought it up to my mom afterward, she confirmed everything the psychic had said.

That moment shook me. It left me with even more questions and a deeper desire to explore the world of the unseen.

This was The Seeking—a time when I was actively searching for pieces of the puzzle, pulling knowledge and insights from different sources in an attempt to make sense of the world around me and my place within it. Each discovery was like lighting a candle in a dark room— illuminating the path forward.

The Integration

Once we begin exploring spiritual ideas and experimenting with different tools, the next phase naturally unfolds: The Integration.

This is where everything we've learned starts to take root in our everyday lives. It's no longer just about seeking—it's about embodying. We begin to weave these truths into the fabric of who we are and how we move through the world.

For many of us, this phase lasts for years—even decades—as we continually work to align our inner landscape with the way we show up in the world.

Integration asks more of us than just understanding. It asks for devotion. This is where we come to realize that spiritual growth isn't a destination—but a lived experience—one that invites us to show up each day with presence and purpose.

For me, this deepened when I began embracing grounding rituals that truly anchored me. Around 2008, I started working with energy techniques inspired by Donna Eden. I explored yoga for a while, but over time, my connection to the sacred became more personal and intuitive.

These days, my daily rhythm blends energy work, Tai Chi, and Qi Gong. Whenever the weather allows, I step outside barefoot—connecting with the earth in a way that brings balance and flow. These embodied practices help me stay centered, even in life's most chaotic seasons.

The stillness that comes with meditation also plays a vital role. Over the years, I've discovered that mindfulness isn't one-size-fits-all. Some mornings, I sit in silence, focusing on my breath or repeating a mantra. Other days, I find peace just by being with the natural world—listening to wind through the trees, watching clouds drift by, or feeling the solid presence of the ground beneath me.

This year, I was gifted a beautiful djembe drum, and some of my most meaningful moments now happen outside—in our grove or the open fields—playing rhythms for Gaia. In those sacred pauses, I feel in tune with the heartbeat of the earth and all living things.

Integration isn't a box we check or a phase with a clear endpoint. It's a lifelong process of infusing our spiritual awareness into every aspect of life—not just changing how we live but transforming who we are.

Each stage of awakening builds on the one before, gradually preparing us for deeper shifts in perception and being. And as we enter the next stage, we begin to explore how healing and self-love open the path to shedding the old—and stepping into the truth of who we're here to be.

The Transformation

At a certain point, all the spiritual knowledge and practices we've gathered begin to transform us. The Transformation stage is where significant inner changes take place. It's a time when we shed old patterns, beliefs, and behaviors that no longer serve us—and embrace new ways of being that align with our spiritual truth. It's an ongoing process that requires healing, self-reflection, and, most importantly, patience.

Transformation can feel like both a breaking and a becoming—a shedding of the old self that once felt safe, and the emergence of a new self that feels true. It's a tender, often challenging process, but one that is necessary for growth.

For me, this transformation was deeply tied to embracing self-love and overcoming the inner battles that had shaped much of my life. My 30s and 40s were a time of intense personal growth. One of the biggest lessons I learned was the importance of self-love. It wasn't an easy process—far from it. I spent years slowly untangling the thousands of automatic negative thoughts (ANTs) that buzzed through my mind each day, relentlessly picking apart my self-worth. Little by little, I learned to quiet those voices—replacing them with kinder, more loving thoughts. It wasn't an overnight change, but a gradual, deliberate shift toward embracing myself fully, flaws and all.

Part of this journey involved healing the inner child and resolving the trauma of my speech disorder. This process felt like peeling away the layers of an onion—each one revealing something deeper that needed to be addressed. It took decades of self-work, but over time, I began to find my true voice. It wasn't until this past year that I felt I had fully stepped into it. The freedom that comes with healing those old wounds is indescribable—and it's one of the most profound gifts that The Transformation has given me.

Of course, this stage wasn't always smooth. There were dark periods too—times when I struggled to open up, to let anyone in. It began when I lost several friends and acquaintances in one year, each newly engaged or married when they passed. It was a devastating time, one that shaped me in ways I couldn't fully understand until much later.

And then came the loss of my beloved dogs, Blu and Peach. That was a turning point—a moment when I recognized how much I had been carrying. The trauma of that year had been buried deep within me, but losing Blu and Peach brought it all to the surface. It was painful—but it was also the beginning of my healing journey.

The Transformation is ongoing, as each day offers new opportunities to grow, heal, and evolve.

The Enlightenment

We begin to experience a profound sense of unity with all existence in the Enlightenment stage. It's not a destination, but an ongoing process—

a way of living from a place of deep connection. In this stage, we come to understand that the journey isn't about perfection, but about presence. Enlightenment isn't an escape from the world—it's a deeper engagement with it. One that honors the divinity within and around us.

Ironically, long before I fully stepped into this stage, I already had a deep, unshakable knowing that we are all one. When I founded my company, 4 Winds of Change, I wrote on my website: "We are all one: one family, one community, one region, and one world." At the time, I didn't have a spiritual practice or framework to explain it, but I simply knew. We are all connected in a way that transcends the physical. It was more than an idea—it was a truth I felt in my bones.

Over the years, my connection to Gaia and nature has only deepened. I feel it every day—whether it's the wind brushing against my skin, as if it's whispering to me, or the way my ears pick up on every subtle sound around me.

But one experience shifted my understanding in a powerful way—That coyote encounter, which I shared earlier, was one of the first moments I truly felt Gaia's presence. It was as if the boundaries between us dissolved, and I could feel the pulse of the earth—the energy of life flowing through everything around me. That connection has never left me. It's something I return to each day, whether I'm sitting quietly in nature or simply listening to the world around me.

This sense of oneness extends beyond nature. I've always known, deep within, that we are intricately connected to Source and to all that is. The phrase "as above, so below" speaks to this truth, though putting it into words is difficult. It's a feeling more than an explanation—a knowing that we are reflections of the divine, that what happens within us is mirrored in the universe, and vice versa.

Perhaps the most recent and profound experience of this unity came in June of 2024, when I experienced my light language activation. It was unlike anything I had ever felt—a moment of pure surrender to the unknown. And yet, I didn't feel fear. Instead, there was a deep trust that this was part of my journey—part of the unfolding of who I am meant to be. This activation opened a whole new level of connection. A reminder that spiritual growth often involves stepping into the unknown with trust. While I'm still uncovering its full meaning, it deepened my sense of unity with the divine.

The Enlightenment stage isn't about reaching a final destination—it's about continually living in this space of trust, connection, and love. It's about knowing that we are one with everything and everyone—that we are part of a divine tapestry that stretches beyond time and space.

This stage is an ongoing process of remembering who we truly are—and living from that truth.

From Awakening to Becoming

Awakening is not a destination but an invitation—a call to uncover the truth of who we are and why we're here. Yet, understanding is only the first step. True transformation happens when we embrace these lessons, allowing them to shape us in ways that ignite our potential and align us with our divine purpose.

This marks the beginning of *Part 2: Transformation and Growth*—a journey of courage, vulnerability, and trust, where we shed old fears, step into our power, and nurture the light within us. Transformation asks us to love ourselves fully—to see our own worth and honor the divine essence we carry. Only then can we shine brightly in the world.

As we take this next step, we explore how self-love becomes the foundation for growth, a guiding force that leads us toward our higher selves.

We've heard the whisper, remembered our truth, and now stand at the threshold of change. The journey inward begins—not as a retreat, but as a reclamation. What we meet in the depths will shape the way we rise.

In the chapters ahead, we begin to transmute insight into embodiment.

We lean into self-love—not as a concept, but as a living, breathing practice.

And as the layers fall away, what remains is our truest light.

PART 2
Transformation and Growth

"Growth requires courage, the courage to break free from fear, to embrace your own light and shadow, and to step beyond the safety of your comfort zone. In that leap lies the transformation you've been seeking."

The Light Within—Awakening to Self-Love

"The greatest journey you will ever take is the one inward. Love yourself fiercely, for your soul depends on it."

For years, I believed that loving myself was a selfish act. I wrestled with guilt every time I chose my own needs, convinced that prioritizing myself was taking something away from others. But over time, I understood a powerful truth: to truly give to others, I first had to give to myself.

I remember one particular moment vividly. I had just declined an invitation to a social gathering because I needed rest. A close friend called me out, labeling my decision selfish. Her words hit me deeply, leaving me questioning whether I was wrong to prioritize myself. Was it truly selfish to rest when I needed it? The guilt was overwhelming until a moment of clarity began to shift my perspective. How could I give my best to others if I was constantly running on empty? That decision, though small, marked the beginning of my journey to self-love.

I came to realize that self-love is not indulgence; it's a necessity. Imagine trying to water a garden with an empty can—you cannot nurture anything if you are depleted yourself. Loving yourself allows you to cultivate the energy, peace, and clarity needed to show up fully for others. The act of honoring your needs is not selfish—it's an offering of your best self to the world.

When I began my own journey, I discovered I was carrying wounds, fears, and deeply ingrained beliefs that had been holding me back for years. That's when I realized: self-love isn't selfish—it's essential.

It wasn't easy; healing rarely is. But as I committed to loving and healing all parts of myself, something extraordinary happened: I began to show up for others in a way I never could before. My relationships deepened, my energy expanded, and my soul felt free.

This chapter is about that journey—about clearing the noise in your mind, opening your heart, and finding peace within.

The Stillness Within—Meditation as the Key to Self-Love

Meditation became a lifeline for me. My mind used to race endlessly—overthinking, replaying past mistakes, and fearing the future. I was caught in a storm of my own thoughts. But meditation became my guide to discovering that place—a calm sanctuary within myself that existed even when my thoughts and emotions were turbulent.

Meditation isn't about controlling your thoughts; it's about learning to sit with them without judgment. It's about becoming the observer of your mind rather than its captive. This practice gave me the space to explore what lay beneath the surface—the fears, the hopes, and the quiet voice of my soul that the noise had drowned out.

Buddha's wisdom resonates deeply here: "No matter what chaos is happening outside, how still can you be within?"

Imagine the ocean. On the surface, the waves are wild, relentless, and constantly in motion. But deep beneath, the sea is still, calm, and unshaken. You are the ocean, not the waves. Your thoughts, like waves rising and falling, may come and go, but they do not define you. Beneath it all, there is a place of stillness—your soul. Meditation helps you return to that place—the quiet center of your soul that always remains, no matter the storm above.

I remember my first attempt at meditation. I couldn't sit still, my mind jumping from one worry to another. I felt like I was failing. But slowly, day by day, I noticed a shift. My thoughts didn't disappear, but they lost their grip on me. I began to feel the calm beneath the chaos.

Breaking Through Fear and Resistance

As I delved deeper into my meditation practice, I began to uncover the patterns and blocks that had kept me disconnected from self-love. The truth is that fear and resistance are our greatest obstacles. Fear tells us we are not worthy, and resistance keeps us from receiving love, even when offered freely.

I began to understand that fear often disguises itself as logic or practicality. "You don't have time to meditate," it whispers. "You're too busy to focus on yourself." These thoughts kept me trapped, believing that the world would fall apart if I stopped to tend to my own needs. But each time I chose to push past the resistance, I reclaimed a part of myself that fear had silenced.

I noticed this not only in myself but in others: we are often so good at giving but struggle to receive.

But true energetic flow requires both. When we block receiving, we interrupt the natural rhythm of love itself—giving becomes draining, and receiving feels unsafe. Restoring this balance begins with honoring our own worthiness.

I'll never forget a moment with a dear friend who brushed off a heartfelt compliment. "Oh, it's nothing," she said, dismissing my words. That moment was a mirror, reflecting how often I had dismissed kindness toward myself. Why was I so eager to offer love but so reluctant to receive it? This realization marked a turning point in understanding how deeply fear and resistance were rooted within me.

Consistency—The Path to Transformation

Meditation, like self-love, is a practice. When I first began, I questioned if it was working. My mind would wander, and I'd feel frustrated. But the key is showing up—day after day, moment after moment.

Dr. Joe Dispenza's words resonated with me: "We perceive only a fraction of reality through our physical eyes." Over time, as I continued to show up, I noticed a shift. The chatter in my mind began to soften. My heart opened. My energy felt lighter.

Then came a breakthrough moment during a guided meditation. I imagined myself as a child, carrying the weight of unspoken fears and insecurities. As I held her in my mind's eye, tears streamed down my face. I felt an overwhelming wave of compassion, as though I was finally permitting myself to love the parts of me I had hidden away for so long. That moment of self-acceptance was transformative.

If you are on this journey, know this: you are worthy of love. Not because of what you do or give to others, but because you are here. Your existence alone is enough.

Integrating Self-Love—Clearing, Receiving, Becoming

Self-love requires us to clear the blocks that hold us back—fear, resistance, and unworthiness. These blocks keep us small, convincing us that our fears and limitations define us. But the truth is, we hold the power to let them go when we turn inward with honesty and love.

It's not about erasing your pain but learning to sit with it, understand it, and ultimately release it. The courage to face these blocks is what sets you free—free to love more deeply, to live more authentically, and to reconnect with the truth of who you are. With every layer you peel back, you rediscover the truth of who you are—a being of infinite worth and love.

Sometimes, these blocks are buried deep in our bodies, in our energy fields. They may come from past experiences, ancestral wounds, or simply the stories we've been told about who we are. But when we do the work—through meditation, healing, and self-reflection—we begin to release them. Ask yourself:

- What fears are keeping me from loving myself fully?
- What resistance do I feel when I try to receive love?
- Where do I feel unworthy, and why?

The answers may not come all at once. Healing is a process. But each time you choose self-love—you quiet your mind, connect with your heart, and release an old story—you take one step closer to your true self.

As I began prioritizing self-love, I noticed subtle but profound changes in how I showed up for others. Establishing healthy boundaries allowed me to be more present and patient, no longer running on empty or feeling stretched too thin. I found myself engaging with loved ones more deeply, offering them the best of me, not just what was left of me.

I leave you with this message, a transmission from my soul to yours: You are worthy. You are enough. Your voice, presence, and light are gifts to this world.

Give yourself the love you so freely give to others. Take time to be still. Quiet your mind. Listen to the wisdom of your heart. In that space, you will find peace. And in that peace, you will discover the infinite love that already exists within you.

Reflective Takeaway

- Self-love is not selfish; it's the foundation for all healing.

- Meditation is a powerful tool to quiet the mind and connect with your soul.
- Consistency in your practice will lead to transformation.
- To open your heart, you must release fear, resistance, and unworthiness.

Self-love opens the door to growth—but with every step toward the light, shadows inevitably rise to greet us. These shadows are not barriers but invitations—challenges asking us to face what we fear most, and reminding us that our next level of expansion often lies just on the other side of discomfort.

As you embrace your light, you'll uncover the strength within to confront these shadows, transforming fear into clarity and courage. It's in this alchemy of love and fear that you discover your boundless potential. The journey forward is not just about releasing fear—it's about reclaiming the life that waits for you beyond it.

From Self-Love to Fearless Becoming

Loving ourselves is how the healing begins. But as we rise into our light, the shadows we once avoided often rise with us. They are not here to stop us—they are here to show us what still needs to be reclaimed.

The next part of the journey calls us to face the fear that's been quietly shaping our lives from behind the scenes. Not to battle it, but to understand it. To walk through it with courage, grace, and the knowing that on the other side of fear lives the freedom to become who we truly are.

Breaking Free—The Courage to Step Into the Light

"Fear is not the enemy—it's the invitation. Step through it, and you'll be free to become who you were always meant to be."

Maybe it's that tightness in your chest when you think about stepping out of your comfort zone. Or that nagging voice in your head whispering, *What if you fail? What if you're not enough?* I've been there. Fear is an unwelcome guest we've all had to entertain at one point or another.

For me, fear began early. As a child, I struggled with a speech disorder that made every word feel like a battle. My second-grade teacher's harsh words—"stupid" and "dumb"—stung deeply and left me questioning my worth for years. Fear kept me small, convinced me I wasn't good enough, and whispered that the world was safer if I stayed in the background.

But here's the thing about fear: it's not the enemy. It's a teacher. It shows up to point out where growth is waiting. Breaking free isn't about eliminating fear—it's about learning to live courageously alongside it.

The Nature of Fear

Fear is an inescapable part of life. It shows up in countless forms—fear of failure, fear of judgment, fear of change. Sometimes, it's a whisper in the back of your mind; other times, it's a full-blown wave of panic. But one thing is constant: fear thrives on control.

In those early years, fear quietly took the lead in my life. It wasn't just the fear of speaking—it was the fear of being seen, of being judged. I built walls around myself, hoping they'd keep me safe. But fear doesn't disappear when you hide. It waits. And over time, I learned that the only way to break free was to face it head-on.

Understanding Fear as a Teacher

Fear isn't here to punish us—it's here to guide us. It shows up when we're standing at the edge of growth, when life is nudging us toward something bigger. But instead of seeing it as an opportunity, we often view fear as a roadblock.

Fear challenges the stories we tell ourselves—about our limitations, our worth, and our potential. It often feels like an insurmountable obstacle, but what if it's simply a test? When fear shows up, it's a sign that something meaningful is at stake. Each time we face it, we rewrite those limiting stories, transforming fear into a catalyst for growth.

In 1983, I found myself thrust into one of the most terrifying moments of my life. I had created a presentation for the president of my company—who also happened to be my father—to deliver at the International Liquid Terminal Association conference. At the last minute, he was unable to attend, and I was asked to go in his place.

The audience was massive—600 professionals—and I was the only woman speaker. Scanning the room, I spotted only a handful of other women among the sea of suits. My hands trembled as I gripped the podium. I could feel my heart pounding in my chest, and every voice of doubt from my past echoed in my mind: What if they think I don't belong here? What if they don't take me seriously?

But as I stood there, something shifted. I realized fear wasn't trying to stop me—it was trying to teach me. It was asking, are you ready to grow? That moment wasn't just about delivering a presentation; it was about reclaiming my voice, stepping into my strength, and proving to myself that I belonged.

Reflecting on that moment now, I realize it wasn't just a lesson for the stage. It was a turning point in how I saw fear—not as a wall but as a doorway to transformation.

Breaking Free—The Journey

Looking back, I now recognize how that moment on stage revealed something I couldn't fully see at the time—it planted the seeds for a deeper understanding of how to move through fear. In hindsight, here's what I see that experience taught me:

Awareness: I can now see that the first step was naming the fear: *I'm afraid of being judged. I'm afraid of failing.* Naming it didn't make it disappear, but it gave me clarity.

Acceptance: I didn't try to push the fear away. My hands trembled, my voice shook—but I allowed myself to feel it. I now know that courage isn't the absence of fear; it's choosing to move forward with it.

Action: The first words out of my mouth were shaky, but I kept going. With each sentence, the fear began to loosen its grip. By the time I finished, I wasn't just delivering a presentation—I was reclaiming my voice.

That moment didn't just challenge me—it became a turning point. Only later did I realize that fear often appears when something meaningful is waiting on the other side.

Through Fear's Doorway—Tools, Truth, and Transformation

Here are some practices I've found helpful in working with fear:

Breathing Exercises

When fear feels overwhelming, pause and breathe deeply. Inhale for four, hold for four, exhale for four. This will calm your nervous system and bring you back to the present moment.

Try this the next time fear arises: Take four deep breaths, as described above, before responding. You may notice your mind clearing and your confidence returning.

Journaling

Write down your fears. Sometimes, seeing them on paper takes away their power. Ask yourself: *What's the worst that could happen?* You'll often find it's not as scary as it seems. *What's the best that could happen?* For me, journaling helped untangle the stories fear was telling me. Once I saw them clearly, I could rewrite them into something empowering.

Visualization

Picture yourself succeeding—not perfectly, but courageously. Imagine being on the other side of fear, feeling proud and strong. While I didn't visualize success before stepping onto that stage in 1983, I *did* use deep breathing to steady myself. That simple act of presence kept me grounded, even as my nerves surged.

Support Systems

Don't be afraid to lean on people you trust. Fear can feel smaller when it's shared. Whether it's a friend, coach, or mentor, having someone remind you of your strength can make all the difference.

And as we begin to walk through it with support at our side, something begins to shift.

Fear often feels like a wall we can't climb. But when we face it, we find it's not a wall at all—it's a doorway.

On the other side of fear lies a version of yourself you've yet to meet—a stronger, wiser, and more courageous self. Every step you take through fear is a step closer to that empowered version of you. It's not just about conquering fear; it's about discovering the resilience that's been waiting within all along.

Standing on that stage, I didn't just conquer a fear—I found a freedom I didn't know was possible. The applause wasn't just for my speech; it was for what that moment represented: years of struggle giving way to strength.

Imagine how your life might change if fear no longer called the shots. Who would you be if fear wasn't whispering, *You're not enough*? The truth is, fear is temporary, but the freedom on the other side is lasting. When you step through fear, you discover the courage, resilience, and power that's been inside you all along.

Soul Reflection

Take a moment to pause and reflect:

- What is one fear that's been holding you back?
- If you moved through that fear, what could be waiting for you on the other side?

- How might your life change if you no longer let fear make your decisions?

You don't have to be fearless to be brave. Courage is simply the decision to move forward, even when fear is present. And when you do, you'll discover a strength within you that's been there all along.

What's waiting for you on the other side of fear? Who are you when fear no longer runs the show? The journey to find out is worth every step.

Each act of courage adds a brushstroke to the masterpiece of your life. When you choose to move forward despite fear, you create a ripple effect—not only transforming yourself but inspiring others to do the same. Courage is contagious, and by stepping into your light, you encourage others to find their own.

Breaking free from fear isn't just about reclaiming your strength—it's about opening the door to a new way of seeing the world. On the other side of fear lies a profound truth: the world around us reflects the divisions within. The light and shadow we witness in life mirror the duality we carry in ourselves.

This duality is part of the human experience—the push and pull between what is comfortable and what calls us to grow. By embracing both light and shadow, we unlock a deeper understanding of who we are. It's in holding these contrasts that we find balance, and through that balance, we begin to heal.

But this duality isn't here to divide us—it's here to teach us. Through the tension of opposites, we discover the beauty of wholeness—not by erasing differences, but by embracing them as essential parts of the greater picture. It's in this dance of contrast that we uncover our deepest truths and step into harmony.

What wisdom awaits when we learn to hold both light and shadow within us? The journey toward inner alignment unfolds one breath at a time.

From Fear to Wholeness

As we move beyond fear, we begin to see life with new eyes. But what we find next isn't all light—it's contrast. The deeper our healing, the more we are asked to hold both shadow and shine. We begin to notice how duality lives not just in the world around us, but within us: love and grief, courage and doubt, faith and uncertainty.

This is where the journey leads next—not into separation, but into integration. Because true unity isn't about choosing sides—it's about remembering that we are both/and, not either/or.

Beyond the Divide—
Finding Unity in Duality

*"The path to unity isn't about escaping duality but embracing it.
Light and shadow dance together to reveal the whole".*

I used to think the world was made up of opposites. Good and bad. Right and wrong. Light and dark. I didn't just believe it, I *felt* it. I lived by it.

At the time, I didn't realize I had been taught to see the world through a distorted lens, one that sorted everything into two neat and opposing categories. This or that. Black or white. Safe or unsafe. Trustworthy or suspicious.

This kind of binary thinking is so deeply embedded in our culture that we rarely question it. We're raised to define things by contrast. Separation is reinforced through language, belief systems, societal roles, and how we construct our identities.

But this worldview comes at a cost.

When we filter life through this rigid either/or lens, we begin to experience ourselves as separate, not only from each other, but also from nature, the divine, and even our own inner truth. We start to feel like we must pick a side or choose a label just to belong. And while that might feel safe or familiar at first, it slowly erodes our connection to self and to source.

We become reactive, fearful, judgmental, and closed off to anything outside of our beliefs. We disconnect from our own wisdom.

The Discomfort of Duality
as a Catalyst for Growth

Duality isn't just an abstract concept; it's deeply personal. It shows up in our most vulnerable moments, in our relationships, in our triggers, and in the places where our inner beliefs clash with external realities.

Many of us were taught to view situations—and even parts of ourselves—as either "good" or "bad." It's a pattern deeply embedded in culture, religion, and education. We judge our thoughts, feelings, and experiences through a moral filter. Am I right or wrong? Am I enough or not enough? Am I succeeding or failing?

This inner dialogue creates a constant pull. We chase what we've been told is good and avoid what we've been taught is bad, often without pausing to ask who decided those definitions in the first place.

But duality also holds a mirror up to our deepest growth. It's often the discomfort, the moments that trigger us, that become our greatest teachers. When we react strongly to something "out there," it almost always points to something unresolved within.

It can be jarring when our carefully curated worldview begins to crack. But when we're willing to pause, to sit in the tension instead of running from it, something begins to shift. We stop labeling our emotions as right or wrong. We start observing instead of judging. We begin to question the roots of our beliefs instead of defending them. And that's when the real shift begins.

As I've said before, the outer world is a reflection of our inner world. When we change the lens through which we see, we also change the world we experience.

It's in this journey that we blossom into the best versions of ourselves.

Why Duality Feels So Uncomfortable

Here's the hard truth about duality: it's not always easy to sit with.

When we start to awaken to the rigid boxes we've placed ourselves in, it can feel like the floor drops out from underneath us. The beliefs we once clung to begin to feel too small. The labels we wore so proudly start to itch. And the roles we played to keep others comfortable no longer fit.

We might feel like we're losing our identity. In a way, we are.

This part of the journey is rarely talked about. It's messy, vulnerable, and deeply personal. As we start to soften our grip on old identities and dualistic thinking, we're left in a space that feels unfamiliar and raw.

Part of what makes this so uncomfortable is the internal split we've been taught to accept as normal—the separation between our mind and body, logic and intuition, doing and being. Many of us were conditioned to trust the mind over the body. To value logic over intuition. To push through instead of pause. But awakening invites us to reconnect with the parts of ourselves we've long ignored—the whispers, the instincts, the inner knowing we were told to dismiss.

Sitting in that discomfort takes courage. It's far easier to run back to what's known than to stand in the fog of the unknown. But this is where healing begins.

Eventually, we begin to see that the pain of duality isn't a punishment. It's an invitation. It's a gentle (and sometimes not-so-gentle) nudge from the soul, calling us home to wholeness.

What we seek isn't out there. It's been within us all along, waiting for us to embrace it.

Duality as a Gateway to Unity

If duality creates discomfort, it's only because it's pointing us toward something deeper—something more whole.

When we awaken to the duality within us, we begin to realize that our triggers and emotional reactions aren't obstacles. They're invitations. The push-pull we feel between extremes is not a sign that we're broken; it's a signal that healing is possible.

Every time we feel torn between opposites—light and shadow, control and surrender, belonging and authenticity—we're being offered a chance to choose differently. To soften instead of judge. To witness instead of resist.

It's easy to forget that contrast is how we come to know what we truly want, what we truly believe, and who we truly are. Without the darkness, how would we recognize the light?

By embracing duality as a sacred teacher, we reclaim our ability to respond from the heart instead of react from the wound. We start to bridge the divide within ourselves, which is the first step toward experiencing unity in the world around us.

This is the alchemy of awakening. This is how the shadow becomes sacred.

Duality in Practice—
Witnessing Without Attaching

Duality often plays out in our minds long before it appears in the outside world. One of the most powerful tools we can develop is the ability to witness our thoughts without becoming attached to them.

This doesn't mean ignoring what comes up or pretending we're unaffected. It means creating space between the voice in our head and the truth in our heart. We observe the pattern instead of reacting to it. We get curious rather than defensive.

For example, when the thought "I'm not good enough" arises, it's easy to spiral into old wounds, shame, or self-doubt. But witnessing invites a pause. Instead of identifying with the thought, we notice it: "Ah, there's that old belief again." We don't try to fix it or fight it—we simply observe it with compassion.

That moment of observation is where the shift begins.

When we create that inner spaciousness, we begin to separate the conditioned mind from our true essence. We're no longer pulled into the storm of right and wrong, success and failure, light and dark. We recognize that we are the one watching the weather, not the storm itself.

This practice isn't about perfection. It's about presence. And the more we practice witnessing, the more freedom we find.

The Great Divide vs. The Great Awakening

As we begin to witness the duality within ourselves, we also start to recognize how deeply it shapes the world around us.

We see it in the news, in politics, in religion, and even in family dynamics. Us versus them. Right versus wrong. Worthy versus unworthy. These divisions are everywhere, and they're not just playing out on a global scale—they mirror the divides we carry within.

This is what I call the Great Divide. It's the collective tension that rises when a society becomes more focused on separation than on connection. When fear drives us to retreat into what feels familiar or "correct," we stop listening. We stop seeing each other. We reduce complex people into simplified categories.

It's a reflection of **subject-object duality**—the belief that I am here, and everything else is out there. That "they" are other. That "I" must defend my ground. This illusion of separation is the root of so much suffering, both individually and collectively.

But within this divide lies a deeper possibility.

The discomfort we feel when the world seems split in two can also awaken us to the truth that something greater is unfolding. As we become more conscious of these patterns— in ourselves and in society— we begin to see that this contrast is not a dead end. It's an opening.

This is the threshold of the Great Awakening.

It doesn't require us to pick a side. It asks us to rise above the illusion of sides altogether. To lean into compassion. To remember that what we judge in others often reflects something unhealed within ourselves.

This is not easy work. But it is sacred work.

Practical Tools for Embracing Duality

Awareness is powerful, but it's just the beginning. To truly work with duality, we need tools that help us pause, soften, and respond—rather than react.

The pause is everything.

When we're triggered, our nervous system moves fast. We instinctively fall back into old stories, patterns, and defenses. But when we learn to pause— even for a few seconds—we interrupt that loop. We create space between the experience and the reaction. And in that space, we get to choose.

Here are a few simple but powerful questions I turn to when I notice myself pulled into duality:

- What story am I telling myself right now?
- Where do I feel this in my body?
- Is this an old belief resurfacing?
- Can I hold both truths without needing to resolve them?

These questions aren't meant to fix anything. They're meant to bring you back to presence—to the awareness that there's more than one perspective, more than one way to see, feel, or be.

Duality doesn't disappear just because we notice it. But when we bring curiosity instead of judgment, something softens. We begin to hold space for multiple truths at once. And that's where transformation begins.

Moving Through Duality— A World of Mirrors

As we begin to recognize the patterns of duality in our lives, something else becomes clear: the world is always reflecting us back to ourselves.

It's not always obvious—or comfortable. But the people who trigger us, challenge us, or even inspire us are often holding up a mirror. They show us something we're being invited to see, heal, or reclaim.

Sometimes what we see is a shadow part, an aspect of ourselves we've judged, hidden, or disowned. Other times, it's a part of our power or beauty that we've forgotten or felt unworthy of owning. Either way, these reflections aren't there to shame us. They're there to wake us up.

I've had moments where I judged someone for being too loud, too much, or too assertive—only to realize later that I had silenced my own voice for years. That judgment wasn't about them. It was about the part of me I had abandoned.

When we begin to see the world this way—as a mirror, not a battlefield—everything changes. Life becomes a series of invitations to return to wholeness. Each trigger becomes a teacher. Each reflection becomes a doorway.

We stop seeing others as "other" and start recognizing them as part of us.

This doesn't mean we excuse harmful behavior or bypass healthy boundaries. It means we become more curious. More compassionate. More willing to pause and ask, "What part of me is being called forward right now?"

Because in the end, duality isn't just about contrast. It's about remembering what we've separated from—and welcoming it back home.

And often, what's been separated isn't an idea—it's an emotion.

The 90-Second Rule— Letting Emotions Flow

I've had moments where the tears came fast and hard—deep, gut-wrenching sobs that felt like they came from somewhere beyond this lifetime. I couldn't always explain them. Sometimes, I didn't even know what had triggered them. But I didn't fight them. I didn't try to make sense of them. I let them come. I breathed through them. And just like that, they passed.

That's when I learned one of the simplest and most powerful truths about emotions: if we let them move, they don't stay forever.

When we experience an emotional reaction—whether it's grief, anger, fear, or even joy—it moves through the body in a very specific way. Neuroscience shows that the physiological lifespan of an emotion is about 90 seconds.

That's it.

If we can simply witness the feeling without attaching to the story, it will naturally rise, peak, and pass. But what most of us do is resist it, judge it, or loop it with our thoughts—which causes it to stick around far longer than necessary.

Learning to let emotions flow means honoring that 90-second window. When a wave comes, we can pause, breathe, and allow it. We can notice where it lives in the body—maybe a tightness in the chest or a lump in the throat—and simply be present with it. Not fixing. Not analyzing. Just being.

The more we practice this, the more we realize we don't have to fear our emotions. We don't have to repress them or perform them. We can allow them to move through us like waves—intense for a moment, but never permanent.

This is emotional freedom. And it begins with presence, not perfection.

The Role of Fear and Love in Awakening

At the heart of every awakening is a choice—fear or love.

Fear contracts. It pulls us into scarcity, separation, and survival. It tells us we are not enough, that we have to prove ourselves, protect ourselves, or pretend to be something we're not in order to belong.

Love expands. It invites us into compassion, connection, and truth. It reminds us that we are already enough—not because we've done everything right, but because we exist.

This isn't a one-time choice. It's a moment-by-moment awareness. And sometimes, choosing love feels harder than choosing fear—especially when the fear feels loud, familiar, or even justified.

But love doesn't mean bypassing pain. It doesn't mean pretending everything is fine. Love means showing up—even when we're scared. It means softening toward ourselves. It means choosing presence instead of panic. Truth instead of performance.

In moments of fear, we can pause and ask: What would love say here? What would love do?

Sometimes the answer is bold. Sometimes it's quiet. But it always leads us closer to the truth of who we are.

Awakening isn't about never feeling fear again—it's about remembering that love is still available, even in the presence of fear.

The Dance of Harmony— From Duality to Inner Voice

Unity is not the absence of duality—it's the conscious embrace of it.

It's the moment we stop trying to divide life into neat categories and start allowing space for complexity. It's not about choosing light over dark, or good over bad. It's about recognizing that both live within us— and that our wholeness includes them all.

This is where healing begins. Not through perfection, but through presence. When we stop rejecting the parts of ourselves we were taught to hide—the fear, the grief, the shadow, the softness—we begin to live from a deeper truth.

Unity doesn't mean everything becomes the same. It means everything belongs.

It means we hold space for joy and sorrow. For strength and vulnerability. For the human and the divine. It's the integration of opposites that reveals our true nature—not one side or the other, but the sacred dance between them.

When we embrace unity through duality, we stop searching for something outside of us to complete us. We begin to see that we were never separate to begin with.

We return to ourselves—and in doing so, we return to each other.

When we stop fighting with ourselves—when we stop needing one part to win over the other—something remarkable happens.

We begin to dance.

Not in the sense of perfect choreography or polished movement, but in the deeper rhythm of life itself. A rhythm where shadow and light move together, where contraction leads to expansion, and where contrast reveals connection.

This is the dance of harmony.

It's not about balance in the way we've been taught—equal parts measured on a scale. It's about listening. Leaning in. Moving with life, rather than against it.

Harmony is alive. It breathes with us. Some days it feels like grace. Other days it feels like surrender. But when we stop needing certainty and allow ourselves to move with what is, we begin to feel the unity we've been seeking all along.

This is what duality teaches us: wholeness isn't perfect, but present. Not fixed, but free.

True harmony isn't found by eliminating conflict—it's found by allowing contradiction to exist without collapse. When we stop needing to choose sides within ourselves, we begin to embody something much deeper than balance. We begin to live as the bridge between worlds.

And from that space—the place where judgment quiets and presence leads—a new voice starts to emerge. One that's been there all along, waiting patiently beneath the noise.

It doesn't demand attention. It invites us inward.

And the more we listen, the more it reveals who we were always meant to be.

And as we listen, something else begins to stir—an awareness not just of who we truly are, but of who we've been pretending to be.

The habits, roles, and stories that once kept us safe start to feel too small. They no longer match the voice rising within.

That's when the real work begins: breaking free from the unconscious cycles that once kept us small, so we can choose—intentionally, soulfully—who we were always meant to be.

But awareness alone isn't enough. To truly reclaim who we are, we must untangle the patterns that have shaped us from the inside out. These are the loops we didn't know we were caught in—the habits of thought, belief, and behavior that quietly defined us.

What happens when we finally hear the voice within... and choose to listen?

From Habit to Harmony—Breaking the Cycle of Who You've Been

"The moment you realize you've been repeating the same thought without question, you reclaim the power to choose again."

There's something subtle that happens when you've lived the same way for a long time—you stop questioning it. The voice in your head becomes familiar, the habits feel automatic, and the emotional patterns seem like facts of life rather than choices. But what if they're not?

What if you're not actually stuck—just rehearsing a version of yourself you've unconsciously memorized?

For years, I believed I was a kind person. And in many ways, I was—supportive, thoughtful, the one others came to for advice. But beneath the surface, there was a voice I wouldn't dare speak to anyone else the way it spoke to me. It was sharp. Critical. Relentless. I didn't even realize it had taken up residence in my mind because it had always been there.

I thought I was just being "realistic" or "motivated." I didn't see the quiet damage being done by a stream of thoughts I had never consciously chosen—but repeated like a script I didn't realize I was still agreeing to.

And then, one day, I noticed it.

Not the whole pattern. Just a moment. A single phrase I said to myself without thinking. And for the first time... I thought, Wait. Why am I talking to myself like that?

That moment of awareness—small as it seemed—was the beginning of everything changing.

The ANT Moment—When I Realized My Thoughts Were on Repeat

I was around 35 when it hit me. Not in some dramatic, life-altering breakdown—but in the quiet realization that the thoughts in my head were not only *repetitive*, but almost entirely *negative*.

I was having one of those ordinary days where nothing was exactly wrong, but everything felt heavy. I was driving, lost in my own head, when I caught a familiar thought floating by—*Damn, why did you say that? You sounded like such an idiot. Next time, keep your mouth shut.*

It wasn't a new thought. It was a regular. A frequent flyer. But for some reason, that day, I heard it differently. It was like someone had turned up the volume.

And that's when I knew: I wasn't just thinking negative thoughts occasionally. I was living inside them.

I'd heard the term before—ANTs, or Automatic Negative Thoughts—but that day, it clicked. These weren't just passing thoughts. They were shaping everything. They show up like uninvited guests, repeating themselves over and over until they become your internal soundtrack. And unless you pause to question them, you start believing they're telling the truth.

But here's the thing: they're not. And the moment you recognize them, you've taken the first step toward choosing a new story.

The Loop That Shapes Your Life

Most people don't realize they're living the same day on repeat. Not because their lives are boring—but because their inner dialogue rarely changes.

It's a loop. One we don't see, but we feel the effects of it every day.

It starts with a single mental script. That repeated message stirs a feeling. That emotion then drives an action—or inaction. And when we keep recycling the same internal narratives, emotional reactions, and behaviors, we start to believe: *This is just who I am.*

Thought → Emotion → Behavior → Identity

For example, a simple belief like *"I'm not good enough"* might spark feelings of insecurity. That emotional state might lead you to shrink in a meeting, hold back in a conversation, or procrastinate on something you care about. When that behavior becomes your norm, it reinforces the idea that you're someone who never speaks up, who always hesitates, who doesn't follow through.

And so, the loop continues.

This was a game-changer for me when I first understood it.

For years, I believed I had to change my circumstances in order to feel better. But it turns out—it's the other way around. When you shift your mindset and emotional state first, the behavior changes. And when your behavior shifts, your life follows.

Dr. Joe Dispenza puts it this way:

"Your personality creates your personal reality."

If you keep thinking the same way, you'll keep making the same choices. And if you keep making the same choices, you'll keep living the same experiences.

The good news? The moment you become aware of the loop... you're no longer trapped in it.

You can choose a new narrative. You can pause before the feeling takes over. You can practice a different behavior—even something small. And in doing so, you begin creating a new version of yourself.

It doesn't have to happen all at once. It happens in micro-moments. Like noticing when your inner critic shows up. Or catching yourself before you slide into autopilot.

Awareness breaks the cycle. Intention builds the new one.

The Science of Change— Becoming Someone New

There's something deeply empowering about realizing you're not stuck—you're just practiced.

Most of us aren't repeating patterns because we're broken. We're repeating them because we've rehearsed them for years. And like anything we repeat enough, they become second nature.

This is where the science gets exciting. Dr. Joe's research shows that the brain is *changeable*—it's designed for rewiring. The term is neuroplasticity, and it means your brain forms new connections every time you learn something new, think a new thought, or experience a new emotion.

When I first learned this, it felt like someone had handed me the keys to a part of myself I didn't even know was locked.

Because if the brain is changeable, that means *I* am too.

The first time I tried to reframe an automatic thought, it felt awkward. Like trying to write with my non-dominant hand. I'd catch myself thinking, *"You're never going to get this right,"* and I'd pause. Instead of arguing with the thought or pretending I didn't feel discouraged, I would gently introduce something different. Even something as simple as, *"What if that's not true?"*

It wasn't about being blindly positive. It was about creating space between the trigger and my reaction. That space—however small—was where something new could begin.

Dr. Joe teaches that elevated emotions—like gratitude, joy, love, and freedom—are magnetic. When we combine them with clear intentions, we begin broadcasting a new energetic signal to the quantum field. We're no longer looping in the past—we're practicing the future.

And that future begins to show up. Not always immediately. But steadily. Subtly. In synchronicities. In opportunities. In the way people respond to us differently, because we're showing up differently.

The change doesn't start "out there." It starts in here.

With one new thought. One elevated emotion. One choice that says: *"I'm no longer rehearsing the version of me I'm ready to outgrow."*

The Practice—Interrupting the Loop

Awareness is the first step. But practice is what creates transformation.

You can know the loop exists. You can understand that you're not your thoughts, and even believe that change is possible. But until you begin to *interrupt* the old patterns and *rehearse* the new ones, life tends to stay... well, familiar.

So how do you do it?

Not with force. Not by bulldozing your way through fear or pretending everything is fine.

You begin with a pause.

Just a breath.

Just a moment between the thought and the reaction.

That's where everything shifts.

Try This: The Loop Interrupt Practice

1. Catch the Thought.
Begin noticing when a familiar script shows up. It might sound like:
"I always mess this up."
"No one really cares what I have to say."
"Why do I even bother?"
You don't need to fix it—just catch it. Awareness is the disruptor.

2. Name the Emotion.
Ask yourself: *What do I feel when I think this thought?*
Is it shame? Frustration? Hopelessness?
Naming it helps you detach from it—it's no longer running the show behind the scenes.

3. Choose a New Thought.
You don't need to leap to the opposite extreme. You just need to introduce possibility.
Try:
"What if this could go differently?"
"I'm learning to trust myself."
"I'm showing up with love, even if I feel unsure."
Let the new thought be believable. Let it feel like a gentle shift, not a forced leap.

4. Anchor into the Body.
Place your hand on your heart. Breathe into it. Feel the rhythm.
This is coherence—the alignment of heart and mind.

Let gratitude or compassion rise, even just for a breath or two.

Each time you practice this, you're not just interrupting a loop—you're forming a new one.

You're teaching your body that safety doesn't come from staying stuck. It comes from presence. From intention. From gently walking yourself toward the person you're becoming.

Living in the Energy of the Future

You don't have to wait for your life to change before you feel differently.

In fact, it's the other way around.

Dr. Joe teaches that the moment you *feel* elevated—before anything in your outer reality shifts—you've stepped into the frequency of your future. In the quantum field, where all possibilities exist, you attract what matches your energetic state. That means the future you desire isn't waiting for you to *get it all right*—it's waiting for you to remember who you already are.

This truth changed everything for me.

There was a time when I thought I had to have the proof—the result, the validation, the outcome—before I could relax, celebrate, or feel like I was enough. But the more I practiced stepping into new energy, the more I began to see that who I *was being* mattered far more than what I was doing.

When I showed up with the energy of trust, things flowed.
When I allowed myself to feel joy—even if there was still uncertainty—more joy came.
When I stopped waiting to *earn* my worth and just embodied it, my outer world began to shift in the most unexpected ways.

You don't manifest what you *want*.
You manifest who you are *being*.

So who are you becoming?

Not the version of you who's trying to outrun fear.
Not the one still carrying old stories like armor.
But the one who remembers. The one who chooses alignment even when it's inconvenient.
The one who feels free *before* the world gives her a reason.

That's when the miracles happen.

Becoming the Future You—Identity, Reflection, and Flow

There's a moment in every transformation where something quietly shifts.
Not with fireworks or grand announcements—but in a breath.
A whisper.
A pause between who you've been and who you're becoming.

It's the moment you catch yourself before you shrink.
The moment you speak up instead of staying silent.
The moment you feel a familiar fear rise—and choose presence instead of panic.

That's the moment you know:
You are not who you were.

You're not the thoughts you once believed.
You're not the loop you repeated.
You're not the old story you inherited or the mask you wore to survive.

You're something far more powerful.

You are the one who notices.

The one who chooses again.

The one who gently interrupts the past and makes space for a different future.

And the more you practice, the more natural it becomes.

This is how harmony is created—not by being perfect, but by being present.

Soul Reflection

Take a few moments and ask yourself:

- What thought have I been repeating that no longer feels true?
- What emotion am I ready to stop rehearsing?
- Who am I becoming when I let that pattern go?
- What's one new thought I can practice today that feels aligned with the life I'm creating?

There's nothing to fix. Nothing to force.

Just one breath.

One new thought.

One moment of choosing to return to yourself.

This is the shift.

This is the harmony.

And it's already unfolding within you.

And when you give yourself that space—when you pause long enough to choose something new—you begin to create a shift that ripples through every part of your being.

Rewiring your thoughts is just the beginning.

Because once you've softened the grip of old patterns, something unexpected happens—space opens up. Space to feel more deeply. To hear the quieter parts of yourself. To move not from habit or fear, but from something much more aligned.

But with that spaciousness often comes a new level of vulnerability. It's unfamiliar to trust a path you can't see. To surrender control when your nervous system is still craving the comfort of the known. It can feel wobbly at first.

But what if that wobble isn't a sign you're doing it wrong... What if it's a sign you're actually *in the flow*?

Up ahead, we'll explore what it means to let go of the struggle—not to give up, but to allow. To dance with the divine rhythm beneath the surface. To trust the wisdom that lives beyond logic.

Because once you stop rehearsing the version of you built on fear... You begin to remember the one built on light.

From Fear to Flow—The Dance of Divine Balance

"True abundance begins not with what you see, but with what you feel—vibrate higher, and the universe will rise to meet you."

Fear has a way of showing up when you least expect it. Earlier, I recounted a conference I spoke at in 1983—a pivotal moment when I was called to step into a space far larger than I felt ready for: delivering a high-stakes presentation at an industry conference, standing before an audience of 600 seasoned professionals. As I took my place at the podium, memories of my second-grade teacher's harsh words—calling me "broken" and "stupid"—flooded my mind.

My hands shook, hidden beneath the lectern, and I could feel the weight of every skeptical glance. For a moment, the fear felt paralyzing, whispering that I wasn't enough. But something deeper began to stir—an inner knowing that fear wasn't my enemy; it was my ally. It wasn't there to stop me but to guide me. I took a deep breath, leaned into the message I'd prepared, and let the energy of the room shift. That day, I discovered the profound harmony between preparation and intuition, between effort and trust. It wasn't just about overcoming fear—it was about learning to flow with it.

Fear as a Teacher

Fear is something we all face. It can feel like a weight pressing down on your chest, a voice whispering, *What if I fail? What if I'm not enough?*

I know that voice well. As a child, I struggled with a speech disorder that made every word feel like a battle. My teacher's cruel words echoed in my mind for years. Fear became my constant companion, whispering that I would never be heard, never be understood. But over time, I realized something: fear isn't the enemy—it's the teacher.

Fear shows up when we're standing at the edge of transformation. It's like a signal flare, highlighting the places where we're about to grow. Instead of seeing it as a roadblock, we can view it as an invitation—a nudge from the universe to step beyond what we've known and into the realm of possibilities.

Manifestation—Feeling Over Form

Manifestation is often misunderstood as visualization—imagining the car, the house, the perfect life. But true manifestation isn't about what you see; it's about what you feel. The universe doesn't respond to mental images—it responds to the energy you embody. And, energy is shaped by emotion.

When you align your emotions with the essence of what you desire, you create a magnetic field of possibility. It's not about *thinking* abundance; it's about *feeling* abundant—trusting that the universe knows how to deliver blessings in ways we can't always foresee.

I've shared the story of standing on that stage in 1983—how it became a defining moment in reclaiming my voice. But what I didn't realize until much later was what was happening beneath the surface.

I wasn't focused on crafting the "perfect" presentation, picturing the applause, or anticipating any outcome. What grounded me was something far more immediate—the importance of what I was sharing. The information was vital. Life-saving. It had the power to protect workers navigating dangerous environments, like confined spaces within dyked areas of tank farms. That purpose became my anchor. I wasn't there to impress—I was there to serve. And in that sincerity, something shifted. The fear began to soften. The energy in the room changed. And the universe responded.

True manifestation begins with energy, not vision. The energetic field you project—through your emotions, your focus, and the energy you choose to embody—becomes the invitation the universe responds to. It's not about seeing it in your mind. It's about feeling it in your body, anchoring it in your heart, and living as if it's already unfolding.

This is the essence of manifestation: it starts with emotion, not visuals. When we focus solely on the form of what we want—a house, a job, a relationship—we limit ourselves. The universe has a way of delivering blessings in forms we couldn't have imagined, often better than anything we could dream up.

Still, for much of my life, I didn't approach life this way. I didn't lead with energy or emotion—I led with structure, logic, and precision. It wasn't that I didn't believe in possibility; I just believed I had to control the outcome to make it happen. I now understand that this was the masculine energy I had learned to rely on—the part of me that felt safer with plans than with flow.

That masculine lens—logic, action, and structure—helped me succeed in a male-dominated industry and deliver presentations to skeptical audiences. It gave me a sense of control and a clear roadmap to follow. But over time, I realized something was missing. My heart felt disconnected. My soul longed for more.

The Divine Feminine brings a different kind of strength—a quiet power that thrives in intuition, flow, and surrender. It invites us to step away from rigid frameworks and into the expansive realm of creativity and trust. Balancing these energies is not about choosing one over the other; it's about weaving them together to create harmony.

That "more" was the Divine Feminine—the energy of intuition, flow, and creativity. Where the Divine Masculine seeks to build and achieve, the Divine Feminine invites us to pause, reflect, and trust. For years, I thought success required me to rely solely on action and strategy. But as I leaned into my intuition, I discovered a more profound truth: true success isn't about doing more; it's about being in alignment.

Practical Steps for a 5D Life

The shift from fear to flow, from control to trust, is a journey. It's not about perfection but about practice—learning to embrace balance in every aspect of your life. Here are some practical steps to help you integrate the harmony of the Divine Feminine and Masculine and align with the higher vibrations of a 5D reality.

If you're wondering what a 5D life actually means, we'll explore that shortly. But first, here are some foundational practices that help you begin living from a higher vibration—no matter where you are on the journey.

Feel Before You Visualize

Manifestation begins with vibration, not vision. For instance, instead of imagining a dream home, focus on the warmth and joy of living in a space that supports your growth. When you connect with these feelings, you align yourself with the energy of abundance. When your emotions become your compass, the universe responds with synchronicities that defy logic. It's not just about creating a better life—it's about stepping into alignment with your soul's purpose.

Release the Form

The universe often delivers blessings in unexpected ways. For example, when I focused on abundance, I never expected the opportunity to teach others what I had learned—but that became a form of prosperity I'd never envisioned.

Nurture Intuition

Take time for stillness. Reflect on moments when your intuition guided you correctly—like knowing to make a particular phone call that led to an unexpected opportunity. The more you trust your inner voice, the stronger it becomes.

Practice Surrender

Surrender isn't about giving up; it's about releasing control. When I stopped trying to micromanage every detail of my life, I found doors opening effortlessly.

Embrace Creativity

Creativity is a direct connection to flow. Whether through art, writing, or even cooking, engaging in creative activities allows you to express your soul and invites alignment.

What is 5D Reality?

A 5D reality refers to a higher-vibrational state of living in which fear, scarcity and control are replaced by love, abundance, and trust. It's about moving beyond the physical and mental limitations of the 3D world and embracing a deeper connection with one's intuition, soul, and the universe. In this state, decisions come from the heart, and life unfolds with grace and synchronicity.

A New Reality—Love, Abundance, and Balance

Imagine a world where fear no longer dictates our choices, where love and abundance guide our actions. Picture a reality where the Divine Feminine and Divine Masculine energies flow harmoniously, like a symphony in perfect tune. In this world, decisions are informed by intuition and logic—where hearts lead and minds execute, creating a balance that feels as natural as breathing.

This 5D reality isn't a far-off dream—it's a possibility waiting for each of us to claim. The shift begins within. As more of us lean into trust over control, flow over force, and love over fear, the world around us transforms.

Standing on that stage in 1983, I didn't just find my voice—I found my strength. Fear, once a paralyzing force, became a guide, urging me to step beyond my comfort zone. It wasn't about silencing fear but learning to flow with it—to let it shape my growth.

That experience became the foundation for everything that followed. It taught me that fear and flow are not opposites—they're partners, each revealing the balance needed to live authentically and abundantly. The gift of being here, in this life, is the chance to embrace that balance and uncover the treasures within our souls.

When we learn to embrace fear and flow as partners, we begin to uncover the gifts hidden within. These gifts—unique to each of us—carry the power to illuminate not only our own lives but also the world around us.

Next, we'll explore how these gifts can spark the light we carry and how embracing them allows us to live in alignment with our highest selves. The journey inward is one of discovery, and the treasures we find are waiting to be shared.

The Radiance Within— Walking with Your Gifts

"True abundance comes when we stop apologizing for our light and start walking with the gifts already within us."

Have you ever dimmed your light to fit into the shadows around you? I remember a time when I stood at the edge of a decision, unsure whether to step forward or hold back. The fear of being judged, of not being enough, felt like a heavy anchor. It's a feeling many of us know well. Maybe you didn't say the words aloud, but you apologized in other ways—through self-doubt, internal judgment, or shrinking back when you were meant to shine.

I know I have.

For years, I carried a quiet fear that my gifts weren't enough—or worse, that they were wrong. I recall one vivid moment in a meeting when my ability to hold multiple perspectives made me hesitate to take a stance. As I spoke, I noticed the furrowed brows of colleagues—and then heard someone mutter, *"Why can't you just pick a side?"* That moment stuck with me. It made me question whether my compassion was a gift... or a weakness.

I've always had a knack for finding the space between opposites—seeing the shades of gray between black and white, intuitively sensing what drives people's hopes, fears, and motivations. But instead of celebrating this as a strength, I often heard: *"You're not taking a stand."*

That stung. Deeply. I started to doubt myself, wondering if my ability to hold space for nuance was something to hide. But eventually, I realized: my compassion and non-judgment weren't flaws. They were part of my brilliance. And the moment I stopped apologizing for them was the moment I began walking with them.

So now I want to ask you: What light within you have you been dimming? And what would it feel like to step into your full radiance?

The Dual Nature of Our Gifts

Each of us carries unique gifts, a blend of talents and traits that shape our contribution to the world. Some are tangible, like a knack for painting or the ability to lead a team. Others are intangible, like deep empathy, resilience, or the power to bring harmony to a chaotic situation. But not all gifts are the same. Some arise from the ego, while others are rooted in the soul.

Ego-Based Gifts—The Shiny Distractions

The world loves to applaud ego-based gifts. Intelligence, charm, ambition, and productivity are celebrated as markers of success. These gifts often bring tangible rewards: the promotion, the applause, the shiny car parked in the driveway. But there's a cost. When we define ourselves by these external markers, we tether our self-worth to fleeting things—things that vanish the moment the spotlight shifts.

Ego-based gifts are tools; they help us navigate the surface of life, much like a compass that works only on land but fails in the depths of the ocean. They point us toward fleeting rewards and validation but cannot touch the deeper truths of who we are—truths that require us to dive below the surface and explore the vastness of our souls.

Soul-Based Gifts—The Timeless Treasures

Soul-based gifts, by contrast, are infinite. They whisper to us in quiet moments, reminding us of our purpose. I remember once sitting in complete stillness during a meditation, overwhelmed by a profound sense of peace. In that moment, the air was still, and I felt a gentle breeze brush my skin as if the universe itself was offering reassurance. I realized how deeply my intuition had been guiding me all along—quietly and consistently—even when I wasn't listening. This was a soul gift in its purest form, not shouting for attention but gently steering me toward alignment and truth. Compassion, creativity, intuition, and love—these are the treasures of the soul. They don't require validation, nor do they fade with time. Instead, they connect us to our highest selves, offering joy and fulfillment that no external reward could ever replicate.

But here's the challenge: Soul gifts are often undervalued. Society doesn't hand out trophies for quiet resilience or deep listening. Instead, we're encouraged to suppress these gifts, to mold them into something more "acceptable."

The result? We lose touch with the very light we're meant to share.

Activating Your Soul Gifts

Release the Chains of the Ego

Where does your sense of worth come from? If it's tied to job titles, possessions, or others' opinions, it's time to let go. Write down three external measures of success that define you—and then imagine letting them dissolve. Who are you without them? That's where your soul begins.

Reflect on moments where external validation defined your decisions. Ask yourself: Did those achievements truly bring me fulfillment, or did they leave me wanting more? This self-inquiry reveals whether you're tethered to fleeting rewards or grounded in a deeper sense of purpose.

Meditate and Reflect

Spend five minutes in stillness. Breathe deeply and ask yourself, "What gift within me feels silenced?" Allow whatever arises to come forward without judgment.

Trust Your Intuition

Intuition is your soul's compass. Pay attention to the nudges and whispers that guide you. Trust them, even when they defy logic.

Celebrate Your Light

Your uniqueness isn't just an accident—it's your power. Imagine a world where everyone unapologetically shared their gifts. What would it look like? More importantly, how would it feel? This vision isn't just a dream—it's an invitation to create a ripple effect of courage and authenticity.

Each of us carries gifts that, like rare and precious treasures, are meant to be shared with the world. But too often, we downplay them, hiding what makes us extraordinary.

One of my most vivid memories of this truth comes from a moment at sea. I was on a trip in Greece on a sailing yacht, with the salty wind tugging at my hair and the rhythmic crashing of waves against the bow filling my ears. The ocean seemed endless, its deep blue surface shifting and heaving under the weight of the stormy skies. The tang of salt lingered in the air, sharp and invigorating. When rough waters drove most passengers below deck, I stood alone at the bow, leaning into the wind and feeling at peace despite the stormy conditions. Suddenly, movement caught my eye. A single dolphin leaped out of the water, its sleek body arcing gracefully through the waves. Then came another, and another, until an entire pod danced in the wake of the bow. Their energy was pure joy, their movements a celebration of life itself.

The beauty of that moment left me breathless—not just because of their elegance but because they seemed to embody something I had been learning: the importance of unapologetically expressing one's light. The dolphins weren't trying to impress anyone or earn approval; they were simply being themselves, leaping through the waves with grace and abandon. Watching them, I realized that we, too, are called to celebrate our light in this way—not as an act of ego but as an offering of joy and authenticity to the world.

So I ask you, what would it look like to leap boldly into your gifts, to trust the rhythm of your soul as those dolphins trusted the waves?

What light within you is waiting to break the surface?

How can you celebrate it and share it with those around you?

Stories of Soul Alignment

The Gift of Intuition

A mentor once told me, "Your intuition isn't broken—it's just waiting for you to listen." Those words became a turning point for me, but it wasn't until I took Sonia Choquette's course, *Sixth Sense Superpower*, that I began to truly understand and trust my inner guidance. Through her teachings, I learned to quiet my overthinking mind and embrace the whispers of my soul. One day, during a moment of stillness, I felt an undeniable clarity—my "ON switch." That moment changed everything. Today, my intuition is my guide, leading me toward alignment and helping me navigate life's complexities with grace.

The Gift of Compassion

Compassion has always been at the core of who I am. Whether it's in my business or my non-profit work, this gift shapes every interaction. I've seen its power to dissolve tension, bridge divides, and create genuine connections. Compassion isn't just a gift—it's a quiet strength, one that allows me to uplift others while staying rooted in my truth.

The Bank of Source

Imagine walking into a vault, not filled with gold but with infinite love, wisdom, and inspiration. That's the "Bank of Source"—a place I've often visited. I remember once, during a particularly challenging period in my life, feeling completely depleted. In a moment of quiet surrender, I sat in meditation and visualized myself opening the door to this vault. What flowed out wasn't tangible, but it was exactly what I needed: a deep sense of calm and an idea that would later become a cornerstone of my work. It reminded me that when we trust in this infinite reserve, life always provides exactly what's needed. This "Bank of Source" is a metaphor for the Divine abundance available to all of us. When we release the ego's scarcity mindset and surrender to life's flow, we gain access to this limitless reserve. It's not about material wealth; it's about living in harmony with your soul and trusting in life's infinite wisdom.

Integrating Your Light—Reflection, Radiance, and Shadow

Every gift—whether rooted in the ego or the soul—has a purpose. The key is discerning which ones serve your highest good. Take a moment to reflect: What gifts have you been hiding or apologizing for? What would your life look like if you celebrated them instead?

Remember, gifts don't have to be grand to matter. Sometimes, the simplest act—like offering a kind word or listening deeply—has the power to shift someone's day or even their life.

Walking with your gifts means embracing your truth unapologetically. It means letting go of the need for external approval and trusting that your light, like the dolphins leaping joyfully in the waves, was always meant to shine. Those dolphins didn't need permission or applause; they simply embodied their essence, reminding us that our gifts are most powerful when expressed freely and authentically. When you trust that your soul is perfectly equipped to fulfill its purpose, you don't just transform your life—you inspire others to do the same.

So here's my invitation to you: Stop apologizing and start walking. The world needs your light now more than ever.

Walking in your light doesn't mean turning away from the darkness—it means inviting it to dance. The interplay of light and shadow shapes the richness of our human experience. Without the contrast, we lose the depth and wisdom both offer. As we delve into the shadows of ourselves, we uncover hidden gifts waiting to be integrated into our light. Just as the sun's brilliance casts shadows, the gifts we carry often illuminate the parts of ourselves we've hidden away. To fully embrace our light, we must also honor the wisdom within our shadow.

As we step further on this journey, we'll explore how the parts of ourselves we once feared or resisted can become allies in our growth. It's in the harmony of light and shadow that we uncover the deepest truths about who we are.

Dancing with the Shadow— Embracing Your Inner Darkness

"When you turn and face the shadows, they stop chasing you."

Have you ever felt an emotion so overwhelming that you pushed it away, hoping it would disappear? Maybe it was anger, jealousy, or fear—those feelings we label "bad" or "unacceptable." But what if those very emotions were trying to reveal something meaningful? What if, instead of running from the shadows within, you turned toward them and said, "I'm listening"?

Our shadows often feel like unwelcome guests, but they hold the keys to parts of ourselves we've been too afraid to explore. Instead of being monsters to vanquish, they're guardians standing at the gates of transformation. When we approach them with curiosity rather than judgment, they can reveal truths we've hidden even from ourselves.

Let me tell you a story about a moment that changed me. A few years ago, I was on a phone call with my dear friend Marian. She was working on a project to move her business forward, and during our conversation, she said something that stopped me in my tracks: "I'll wait for you to finish updating your course before I move forward." At the time, I was revising a course on using a specific platform for your website and sales funnels. While the updates weren't complete, the existing content was perfectly sufficient for her to get started. Her words struck a nerve. In an instant, I was furious.

In that moment, something inside me flared. I responded with frustration—more sharply than I wish I had. Looking back, I can see that her words touched a nerve I hadn't fully acknowledged.

That exchange stayed with me, not because of what she said, but because it revealed a part of myself I'd been avoiding: my fear of failure and my pattern of delaying out of a need for perfection. Her words were a mirror, offering an unexpected truth I hadn't wanted to see. That moment became a catalyst—not for disconnection, but for deeper self-inquiry. And for that, I'm grateful.

The Gifts Within the Darkness

Here's the secret no one tells you: your shadow holds gifts. That anger you've been suppressing? It might be trying to show you where your boundaries have been crossed. The envy you feel when you see someone else succeed? It could point you toward a dream you've been too afraid to pursue.

Even the emotions we fear most carry profound wisdom. Fear, for example, often signals that we're standing on the edge of growth. It whispers, *You're about to enter the unknown.* When we stop running from these feelings and start asking what they have to teach us, we find pathways to deeper self-awareness and healing.

For years, procrastination was my shadow. I hated how it made me feel—trapped, frustrated, and unable to move forward. It was a cycle I couldn't seem to break, no matter how much I tried. Today, I realize that my experience with Marian began a new journey for me. It was the day I started to work through my shadow, and I began to see the truth: procrastination wasn't a flaw; it was a symptom. Beneath the surface, it was rooted in my fear of imperfection. I was so terrified of not getting things "right" that I'd convince myself to wait, to delay, to avoid trying at all.

When I began to see procrastination as a teacher rather than an enemy, it transformed. That fear of imperfection? It was also a deep desire for authenticity and excellence. By embracing the shadow, I learned to approach my work with greater curiosity and self-compassion. I started taking small, imperfect steps, trusting that the process mattered more than perfection.

The shadow isn't here to sabotage you. It's here to help you grow. When we stop resisting the darkness and start listening to it, we uncover strengths we never knew we had.

How to Dance with the Shadow

Get Curious

Ask yourself, "What is this emotion or trait trying to teach me?" Instead of labeling emotions as "bad," explore what they might reveal about your unmet needs or desires.

Examples of Shadows:

- *Fear of Rejection:* Many of us go out of our way to avoid conflict or disappointment, often saying 'yes' when we want to say 'no.' This shadow might manifest as people-pleasing, which feels like a kindness on the surface but often leads to resentment. Beneath this lies a deep longing for acceptance and the fear of being seen as 'not enough.' By facing this shadow, you can learn to set boundaries with love and prioritize your needs without guilt. It's not about rejecting others but about accepting yourself fully.
- *Suppressed Anger:* From a young age, we're often told, 'Don't be angry; it's not nice,' or 'Stay calm, don't make a scene.' Over time, this can lead us to bottle up anger, believing it's unacceptable or harmful. But anger, when acknowledged, is actually a powerful signal. It often arises when our boundaries have been crossed or when something deeply important to us has been threatened. By

facing and working with this shadow, anger can become a source of energy, clarity, and even courage to stand up for what matters most.

Practice Self-Compassion

Treat your shadow with kindness. Recognize that you're not broken— you're evolving. Offer yourself the same understanding you would extend to a close friend.

Use Reflection Tools

Journaling is a powerful way to explore your shadow. Start with prompts like:

- What triggers me, and why?
- What am I most afraid to admit about myself?
- How might this shadow trait be a hidden strength?

Seek Support

You don't have to navigate shadow work alone. Trusted friends or mentors can hold space as you reflect—not to dwell in old stories, but to witness what's ready to be seen and released.

The goal isn't to rehash the past or get stuck in the wounds—it's to move through them with compassion, clarity, and grace. When support is rooted in growth and alignment, it becomes a bridge between who you've been and who you're becoming.

Remember, shadow work isn't about living in the dark—it's about integrating all parts of yourself so you can rise into wholeness and move forward with power and presence.

Philosophical Insights

Shadow work is not just about personal healing; it's about understanding the broader forces that shape who we are. By looking at how our shadows are influenced by societal norms and the interplay of light and darkness, we gain a deeper appreciation for the transformative power of this journey.

When we work through our shadows, we're not just healing ourselves—we're breaking cycles. We're unlearning the patterns handed down by generations before us and choosing to show up differently. Each time we integrate a shadow, we're planting seeds of wholeness for future generations.

- *The Role of Societal Conditioning:* From a young age, we're taught to fit into boxes designed by societal norms. *"Boys don't cry." "Good girls are quiet." "Success is measured by productivity."* These messages shape how we see ourselves and others. In the process, traits like vulnerability, creativity, and rest are often pushed into the shadows.

  But these aren't just personal shadows—they're cultural and generational ones, passed down through families, institutions, and lineages. When we engage in shadow work, we're not only healing ourselves—we're disrupting inherited patterns and freeing future generations from cycles that no longer serve. In this way, shadow work becomes both a personal act of liberation and a quiet rebellion against the limitations society has placed upon us.

- *The Paradox of Light and Shadow:* Shadows exist because of light. Just as the sun casts shadows in the physical world, the brighter your inner light, the more defined your shadows can become. This paradox is at the heart of shadow work: the very traits we fear and suppress are often the ones that reveal our deepest truths and most profound strengths. Shadow work is a dance between these polarities—a way of harmonizing the light and the dark within us, so neither dominates but both are embraced.

Integrating the Shadow—Missteps, Reflection, and Wholeness

Avoiding Extremes

One common mistake is over-identifying with the shadow. Yes, your shadow is part of you, but it's not all of you. The goal is integration, not obsession.

Rushing the Process

Shadow work isn't a one-time event. It's a journey. Be patient with yourself. Growth takes time, and healing unfolds in layers.

Take a Moment to Reflect

What part of yourself have you been afraid to face? What might happen if you stopped running from it and started listening instead? Imagine standing in front of a mirror, looking into your own eyes, and saying, "I see you. I accept you."

One of the most powerful exercises I've ever done involved visualizing my shadow as a figure in front of me. I pictured it as a younger version of myself, scared and misunderstood. When I extended compassion to that version of me, something shifted. The fear dissolved, and in its place, I found strength.

Dancing with your shadow is not about defeating it. It's about learning its rhythm and finding harmony between light and dark. When you embrace the fullness of who you are, you unlock a deeper level of freedom and authenticity.

So, what would it look like to invite your shadow to dance? To move with it instead of against it? To honor the lessons it brings without letting it define you?

From Inner Listening to Embodied Truth

Now, as we continue the journey through transformation and growth, this inner work becomes more than reflection—it becomes embodiment. The harmony we cultivate within expands outward, inviting us to speak, lead, and live from our deepest truth. When we stop hiding our light and start listening to our soul's voice, something powerful begins to rise.

The Voice That Invites Me to Grow

"The voice that calls you to grow will rarely shout—
but it will never stop speaking."

I used to flinch at the word *trigger*. It always felt sharp. Reactive. A sign that I hadn't done *enough work* or that something in me was still too fragile. When something stirred discomfort—a comment, a glance, an unexpected tone—I'd immediately begin the internal investigation: *What is this about? What memory is this pulling from? Why am I like this?*

It was exhausting.

But I now realize I was looking at it all through the lens of self-correction instead of self-compassion. The voice inside me wasn't always harsh—it was trying to grow. And when I stopped labeling these moments as "triggers" and started calling them "opportunities for growth." Something softened.

The moment didn't change. But my relationship to it did.

And that shift made space for a deeper truth to emerge.

There's a voice that shows up whenever I offer something from the center of my heart.

It whispers:
You just want attention. You're doing this for yourself. No one asked you to do this.

I hear it loudest when I pour myself into what matters—when I cook for people I love, create beauty from chaos, or hold my family together in the midst of loss.

That voice isn't new. It's ancient.
It sounds like fear. But it wears the mask of criticism.

And I know where it came from.

That voice was born in the spaces where I felt unseen—where expressing myself was met with misunderstanding or mockery. In those early years, it felt safer to disappear than to risk being rejected.

So when I am seen now—when I take up space—it activates that same voice:
Be careful. They'll think you're too much. They'll leave. You're safer when you're small.

I used to believe it. I used to shrink.

But now... now, I'm learning to meet that voice with something new.

A quieter voice.
One that says: What if you're allowed to be fully here? What if your offering is enough—without explanation, without shame?

The Reframe—From Reaction to Invitation

"Triggered" sounds like something happening *to* me.

"Opportunity for growth" feels like something unfolding *within* me.

That one shift in language opens up an entirely different kind of conversation with myself—one that feels rooted in sacred curiosity, not self-blame.

Instead of spiraling into self-doubt, I can pause... and ask:

- What is this moment really about?
- What is being asked of me here?

- What part of me is ready to be seen?

It's not about bypassing the hard emotions. It's about listening to them differently.

The Voice That Said—
"You Don't Do Enough"

There's a voice that returns in the quiet hours—the one that tells me I don't do enough. That working from home isn't real work. That what I offer doesn't count unless it's paid for or praised.

But this voice forgets the groceries. The early mornings. The details I remember before anyone asks. The land I tend. The family I anchor. The countless invisible acts of love that keep everything moving while no one's watching.

And that voice? It doesn't just show up in the present—it echoes from childhood. From classrooms. From every moment I felt unseen. From every time I spoke and wasn't heard—or wasn't expected to speak at all.

But I hear me now.
And that's a beginning.

The Sacred Pause—
Meeting Fire with Stillness

There is power in the pause.

In that moment—right before the story spins, before the armor goes up—you can catch a breath. Not always. Not perfectly. But sometimes. And that's enough.

That breath is where the opportunity for growth lives.

It's not glamorous. Sometimes, it's messy and shaky and silent. But it's the birthplace of a new voice—the one that says:

You don't have to protect yourself here.
You get to meet yourself here.

I learned this in the hardest way.

There was a time when words that felt like attacks—whether subtle or direct—would send a lightning bolt through my body.

It didn't matter if they came from a stranger, a parent, or a partner. Something deep in me would ignite, fast and hot, like a warning siren going off. It wasn't just anger. It was furious anger. Rage that had been building over years of being spoken to in ways I didn't deserve—but didn't yet know how to refuse.

And then one day, something shifted.

It wasn't because the voices outside me stopped. It was because the voice inside me finally said:

This is not who I want to be.

Not anymore.

So I paused.
Not to suppress. Not to surrender.
But to breathe.

Thirty seconds. That's all.
Long enough to not match the energy.
Long enough to choose a different voice.

I would say, gently but firmly:
I love you very much. But when I'm spoken to like that, I need to leave.

And then I'd walk away.
Not in silence. Not in shame.
In clarity.

That pause became sacred.
A place of self-respect.
A quiet revolution that let me meet fire with stillness—and still stand in my power.

The Gift Inside the Discomfort— Reclaiming Our Inner Voice

No one signs up for pain. But the discomfort we avoid often holds the most sacred invitations.

Sometimes, it's not the person in front of us who needs our attention— it's the voice inside us whispering, *Do you see me yet? Do you love me here, too?*

Over time, I've come to trust that the moments that make me ache the most are often the ones stretching me into my wholeness.
It's uncomfortable. But it's not unkind.
It's a kind of growing pain that leaves wisdom in its wake.

I remember the moment I finally said enough.
After years of absorbing criticism that wasn't mine, of holding space for someone else's pain while silencing my own, I stood up—not to fight, but to claim myself.

I knew the pain being projected at me wasn't really about me. But even understanding that didn't make the words easier to bear.

For years, I stayed silent.
Until I couldn't anymore.

I didn't scream. I didn't run.
I just stood still and said:
I won't be spoken to like this anymore.

And something shifted.
Not outside of me—but within.

That was the first time I met a version of myself who could hold boundaries and compassion in the same breath.
She is still with me.

This isn't about spiritualizing suffering.
It's about reclaiming it.

It's about naming discomfort not as proof we're failing, but as evidence that we're still becoming.

You'll still have moments when you feel the sting.
But instead of shrinking, ask:

What's trying to grow here?
What am I being invited to see?
What truth is rising up in me that's ready to be honored?

That's the voice I want to listen to now.
The one that doesn't shame me for feeling—
But invites me to heal through it.

Soul Reflection

Think back to a recent moment when something stirred emotional discomfort.

Rather than asking, *Why did this trigger me?* Try approaching it with gentler curiosity:

- *What is this offering me?*
- *What truth is this revealing about where I'm ready to grow?*
- *What voice within me is asking to be heard—maybe for the first time?*

There's wisdom inside the ache.

When we pause to listen, we often find not just pain, but presence.

From Inner Listening to Global Rising

As we explored throughout Part 2, growth doesn't always begin in the light. It often begins in the shadows—in the quiet discomfort, the stories we've avoided, the parts of ourselves we were taught to hide. But something powerful happens when we choose to stay. To listen. To love ourselves there.

That kind of healing doesn't stop at the personal level—it ripples outward.

Because when we reclaim the fullness of who we are, we begin to show up differently in the world. We lead with heart. We create from truth. We see others through the lens of compassion instead of comparison.

And that is where real change begins.

As we enter *Part 3: Ascension and Connection*, we step into a higher perspective—one that lifts us from the inner work of healing into the sacred work of contribution. What once felt deeply personal now reveals its collective purpose.

The awakening isn't just yours.

It's ours.

And the journey is only just beginning.

PART 3
Ascension and Connection

"Connection is the bridge between the seen and unseen, between the self and the divine. When you awaken to the sacred threads that bind us all, you rise to your highest potential."

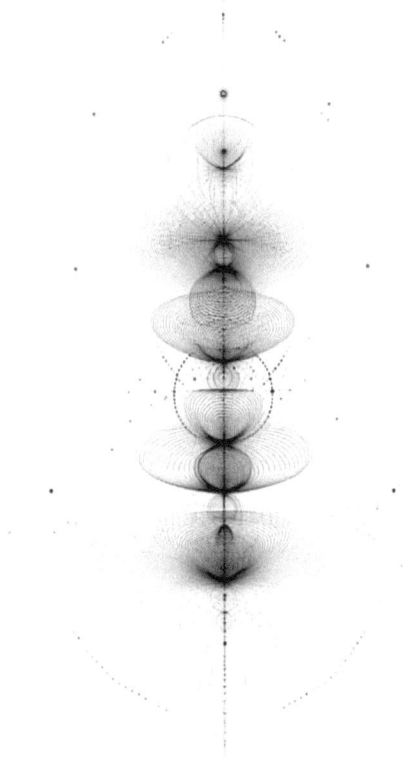

The Call to Rise—Awakening Your Divine Potential

"Awakening is not about becoming something new; it's about remembering who you've always been."

What if the challenges you face are not obstacles but invitations to rise? Invitations to grow, to align with your truth, to step into your highest potential.

Each challenge carries a message, urging us to look deeper within ourselves. What seems like a roadblock often holds the keys to unlocking parts of our potential we've long ignored. These "invitations" are sacred nudges from the universe, reminding us of our strength and capacity to rise.

Imagine for a moment that every setback, every painful experience, is here to remind you of your innate power—your divine essence and sovereignty.

The Great Awakening is more than a buzzword; it's a profound shift, both personal and collective. It's a call to rise above fear and illusion, to reclaim your authentic self, and to step fully into the light of your divine potential. It's not a one-time event but an unfolding journey—one that asks you to shed layers of conditioning and embrace the truth of who you are.

Awakening is not a single moment—it's a journey. A deeply personal one.

For some, it begins with a sudden realization—that life as they've known it no longer aligns. For many, this shift feels like standing at the edge of a cliff, unsure whether stepping forward will lead to a fall or a flight. But awakening is not about having all the answers—it's about trusting that the step itself will reveal the path.

For others, awakening unfolds slowly, like a sunrise gradually illuminating the horizon. But at its core, it is a remembrance: a reconnection to your divinity and sovereignty as the conscious creator of your life.

I remember a pivotal moment in my own journey. There was a time when I felt stuck in a cycle of striving for external validation, believing that my worth was tied to my accomplishments. But something shifted when I began to question those beliefs. Was this truly my path? Or was I living according to someone else's expectations? In that moment of clarity, I realized I had been giving away my power—forgetting that I was already whole, already divine, just as I was. That realization was the first step toward reclaiming my sovereignty.

Awakening is rarely easy. It often begins with disillusionment—a sense that the foundations of your life are crumbling. You might find yourself questioning long-held beliefs, feeling disconnected from what once brought you comfort, or yearning for something more meaningful.

This can feel isolating, but it is also an invitation to rebuild from a place of truth. The pain of disillusionment is not a sign that you've failed; it's a signal that you are shedding what no longer serves you. As the old falls away, it makes space for something far greater: your true self, waiting to emerge. The journey asks you to embrace both your light and your shadow, to integrate all parts of yourself, and to rise into the fullness of who you are meant to be.

Recognizing Your Potential

Before you can rise into your highest potential, it helps to understand what might be holding you back.

Fear of judgment, imposter syndrome, and self-doubt are some of the most common barriers. They whisper, "Who do you think you are?" and "You're not ready." But here's the truth: those voices are not your own. They're echoes of conditioning—remnants of a world that's afraid of your light.

What if, instead of shrinking in the face of those fears, you reframed them? What if challenges were not meant to stop you but to guide you? Think of fear as a compass, pointing directly at what matters most to your growth. It's not here to defeat you; it's here to direct you.

Every challenge carries within it the seed of transformation, waiting to bloom when you choose to face it head-on. For example, a failure might be pointing you toward a path more aligned with your soul's purpose. A painful experience might be the mirror you need to see where healing is required.

Acknowledging your divinity and sovereignty is a crucial step in this process. When you remember that you are a divine being— inherently worthy and infinitely capable—those barriers begin to dissolve.

Claiming your power means recognizing it comes from within—that you are the author of your story. When you stand in that truth, you begin to see challenges not as obstacles, but as opportunities for growth.

Sovereignty is more than an abstract concept; it is a way of living. It shows up in the small moments when you choose your own path, even if it goes against the expectations of others. It's the act of speaking your truth, honoring your boundaries, and creating a life that reflects your values.

For example, when you say "no" to something that doesn't align with your purpose, you are reclaiming your sovereignty. Each time you make a choice from this place of authenticity, you affirm your power as the creator of your own story.

Rising to your potential requires courage. It's about taking imperfect steps forward, trusting that each step will reveal the next. Your intuition is your compass, and your inner light is your guide.

Tools for Rising to Your Highest Potential

Self-Inquiry Practices

Reflection is a powerful tool for awakening. Ask yourself:

- What lights me up?
- What do I feel called to do, even if it scares me?
- How can I align my life with my values and purpose?
- In what ways am I reclaiming my sovereignty?

These questions invite you to go deeper, to connect with the truth of who you are and what you're here to do.

Visualization Exercise

Take a moment to close your eyes and imagine your highest potential self.

What does that version of you look like? How do they feel? How do they move through the world?

Now, imagine that this version of you has been with you all along, quietly waiting for you to notice. The vision you see is not someone you are becoming—it's someone you already are.

Visualize yourself stepping into that version of you with confidence and grace. See yourself embodying your divinity and sovereignty, shining brightly, unafraid of your own light

Trusting the Process

Rising into your potential is not a linear journey. Some days, you'll feel aligned and unstoppable. Other days, self-doubt may creep in—and that's okay.

Trust the process. Every step, no matter how small, brings you closer to the truth of who you are.

Awakening as a Collective Experience

While awakening is deeply personal, it's also a collective experience. As you rise to your potential, you contribute to the awakening of humanity. Your courage to rise becomes a beacon for others, showing them what's possible when we step into our light.

Imagine your transformation as a single candle lighting a dark room—it illuminates not just your path, but the paths of those around you. Your light inspires others to step into their own truth. When you embrace your divinity and sovereignty, you show others what's possible.

Our awakening is interconnected. When one of us rises, we all rise. This is the ripple effect of transformation. Imagine a world where each person remembers their divine essence and fully accepts their sovereignty—a world where fear no longer rules, unity replaces division, and love becomes the guiding force.

In that kind of community, each person stands fully in their light, contributing their unique gifts to the whole. One person's courage inspires another to do the same, creating ripples that extend far beyond the individual. When we choose love over fear, compassion over division, and unity over separation, we co-create a world that reflects humanity's highest potential.

This is the power of collective awakening: a movement that begins within but transforms everything it touches.

Soul Reflection

As we close this chapter, I invite you to reflect on your own awakening journey. Ask yourself:

- What have I awakened to recently?
- How can I step more fully into my gifts?
- In what ways am I honoring my divinity and reclaiming my sovereignty?
- Who am I becoming as I rise to my highest potential?

These answers are your guideposts—leading you to a life that reflects your heart, whether that means creating change in the world or simply showing up fully for those you love.

As we rise into our highest potential—individually and collectively—we become part of something far greater than ourselves. Every act of courage, every choice to honor our truth, becomes a light for others. The journey continues not only within us, but through us... guiding the way forward.

In the next chapter, we'll explore the codes of awakening hidden within our current shift—what it means to live through the Great Transition, and how we can meet it with grace, sovereignty, and trust.

The Awakening Code—Navigating the Great Transition

"There comes a time when we realize we were never lost—we were simply being guided home in a language our soul could understand."

Astrology has fascinated me since my teenage years, ever since a close family friend introduced me to the subject. Their passion for the stars and planetary movements ignited my curiosity, leading me to explore astrology on a deeper level.

Over time, I sought out readings and interpretations of my birth chart, always intrigued by the wisdom the cosmos seemed to hold. My understanding deepened through insights about my Sun, Moon, and Rising signs, yet there was one piece of the puzzle I had never fully grasped—until 3:33 AM, when I experienced a personal awakening that brought my entire path into focus.

I woke up with an unmistakable sense that I needed to listen to a particular podcast episode. I had been following Emilio Ortiz's show for a while, finding value in many of his discussions, but this episode felt different. His guest, an astrologer, spoke about the North Node not just as another point in the chart, but as a map of the soul's evolutionary path.

As I listened, something within me stirred—a deep recognition, as though I had been handed the key to a question I didn't know I had been asking. When I looked up my North Node—Virgo, 12th House—everything about my journey suddenly made sense. The doubts I had carried about my work, the questioning of whether I was truly on the right path, all dissolved in that moment of clarity. I realized that my calling—helping others understand and navigate their awakening—was written in the stars all along.

That realization was so profound that I knew it had to be included in this book. More than that, it had to be part of my upcoming course on aligning spirituality with business. Understanding one's North Node brings immense clarity about what we are here to offer the world—and I knew this was something others needed to discover for themselves.

The Great Initiation: Humanity's Shift in Consciousness

Just as we each have a soul path to walk, the collective is on a journey too. The world is undergoing a profound shift—not just societal or political, but a change in consciousness itself.

People are waking up to a deeper awareness, sensing that the old structures are crumbling and a new way of being is emerging. Many feel it on an intuitive level. They experience restlessness, uncertainty, or an unshakable feeling that they are meant for something *more.*

They are questioning the status quo, seeking deeper meaning, and longing for connection beyond the material world.
This is not a crisis.
It's an initiation.

The discomfort so many are feeling is not a breakdown—it's a sign of the soul awakening to its greater purpose.

Astrology as a Cosmic Roadmap

Astrology offers us a compass in this fog. Not as something to predict or define us—but to *guide* us.

The North Node, in particular, serves as a personal beacon, pointing toward the lessons we are here to embody. It reveals the energies our soul must develop in this lifetime, while the South Node represents patterns, tendencies, and gifts from the past—some of which we are meant to outgrow.

Think of it like this:

- The South Node is the familiar shore.
- The North Node is the wild, unknown sea your soul longs to explore.

Living in alignment with your North Node doesn't mean abandoning who you've been—it means expanding into who you *truly are.*

The Transition from the Piscean Age to the Aquarian Age

Astrologically, humanity is transitioning from the Piscean Age to the Aquarian Age.

- The Piscean Age emphasized hierarchy, religious dogma, and looking to external authorities for truth.
- The Aquarian Age calls us inward—to self-sovereignty, innovation, and direct access to Source.

You may have noticed this shift within yourself. You no longer resonate with top-down leadership, you crave truth over tradition, and you feel more drawn to inner alignment than external validation.

This is the Aquarian voice waking up in you.

Understanding Your North Node as a Spiritual Guide

Your North Node is a blueprint for your highest potential.

When I first began writing this book, I felt called to make the path of awakening feel real, relatable, and within reach—so that anyone, regardless of where they were on their journey, could feel its presence in their own life. But underneath that calling, a question kept rising: *Who am I to teach this?*

That doubt, I later realized, was a whisper from my South Node in Pisces—a past-life imprint of staying small, blending in, dissolving into the background. But my North Node in Virgo, placed in the mystical 12th house, was inviting me to rise. To structure the sacred. To bring the intangible into form. And every time I write and share this wisdom in a grounded, practical way, I align more deeply with my soul's design.

If you've ever felt a calling and doubted whether you're "qualified" to fulfill it—know that your North Node holds a message for you.

I know that feeling well.

Last October, I truly thought I was done guiding others in how to embrace online marketing for their businesses. I was ready to step away—disillusioned by the traditional marketing world. It felt disconnected—too much push, not enough presence. I had no desire to share strategies that felt out of alignment with my spirit.

Then one day, during a phone conversation with JJ Brighton, she paused and said, *"You might be exactly what my clients need."* She was preparing to launch the Lightworkers Expansion Lab and sensed I could play a meaningful role in supporting her community. I wasn't sure what she saw in me—but something about her words landed.

I sat with it. I felt it's truth. And I realized... she had named something I hadn't yet claimed. I wasn't meant to walk away from this work—I was meant to return with a new frequency. One where business and spirituality could finally meet.

Now, I guide women at all stages of awakening—some building soul-led businesses, others simply learning to live more aligned with their truth.

It turns out, my North Node had been guiding me all along. Not back—but forward into a more sacred way of leading.

Embracing Your Role in the Awakening

As we navigate our personal awakenings, many of us start to wonder: *What is my role in this collective transformation?*

You don't need to be a teacher, healer, or guide in a traditional sense to make an impact. You simply need to show up—authentically, presently, and willing to share what you've learned from your own walk through the fire.

Sometimes, the most powerful thing you can do is speak your truth at the right time to the right person.

Sometimes, it's living your values quietly but consistently.

Sometimes, it's just saying: *I've been there too.*

We are not here to be perfect. We are here to be *real.*

Every time you say yes to your evolution, you help shift the collective forward.

We are the way-showers.

We are the midwives of a new consciousness.

Free Will and the Choice to Evolve

Awakening is not something that happens *to* us. It is a sacred *yes* we offer the universe.

The signs, synchronicities, and inner knowings will come—but we must choose to listen. Distractions will always be there—old patterns, external pressure, and fear dressed up as logic. But once we see them for what they are—fear in disguise—we can return to our truth.

Tools to Stay Centered in Your Awakening:

Meditation & Stillness
Take 5–10 minutes daily to breathe and listen. Your inner wisdom is always speaking—stillness is how we hear it.

Nature & the Elements
Let nature be your recalibration. Walk barefoot. Sit under the moon. Listen to the wind. These moments tune you back into your soul.

Astrology & Self-Knowledge
Study your North Node and track your growth. You are part of a greater cosmic rhythm. Journaling your reflections can help deepen awareness.

Discernment & Boundaries
Your energy is sacred. Learn when to say no. Protect your space. Say yes only when it nourishes or expands you.

Embodying Your Wisdom
Insight is not enough—embodiment is the path. Let your spiritual truths become everyday practices, woven into the way you speak, serve, and live.

The Call to Action—Why You Are Here

If you're reading this, it's not by chance.
You are here for this moment.
This time. This transition.

You don't need to have it all figured out. You only need to *begin*.

Rather than asking, *"Why is this happening?"*, the real question becomes:

"How can I serve with what I already know?"

Your North Node is the compass.
Your soul is the map.
And your next step is the one that matters most.

The path is calling.
Not because you need to become someone else—
but because you are finally ready to remember who you've always been.

Will you answer?

As more of us begin to listen to the quiet inner call and choose evolution, we align not only with our soul's journey—but with the greater rhythm of the universe itself.

In the next chapter, we'll explore what this transition means on a planetary scale. The Aquarian Age is no longer a distant concept—it's here, reshaping how we live, lead, and awaken. Together, we'll uncover what it means to step into this new era with grace, purpose, and vision.

The Aquarian Shift—Embracing a New Era of Transformation

"When the stars shift, and the foundations tremble, we are reminded that transformation begins within. The cosmos and our consciousness are one."

What if the stars themselves were asking us to change? Pluto's entrance into Aquarius signals not just a new astrological era, but a profound call to transform both ourselves and the world we live in.

Every so often, the cosmos nudges humanity into a new chapter. One of those moments is upon us now. Pluto, the planet of death and rebirth, has entered Aquarius, marking the beginning of a transformative 20-year era.

Pluto pushes us to confront the shadows—both within and around us—breaking down what no longer serves so that something new can emerge. In Aquarius, that focus shifts to innovation, collective awakening, and the dismantling of outdated power structures. Together, these energies create a powerful invitation for humanity to step into unity consciousness and awaken to our inherent divinity.

This awakening isn't just for those attuned to spiritual practices—it's a global phenomenon. We see it in how communities are reimagining outdated systems, how individuals are choosing to live with more purpose, and how even the Earth herself seems to be calling us into remembrance.

The Aquarian energy doesn't whisper; it roars. It asks us to embrace collaboration without losing individuality, to build rather than destroy, and to trust the process of collective growth—even when it feels uncertain.

And when I speak of divinity, I don't mean something distant or unattainable. I mean the profound ability we each carry to transcend the limitations we once believed were fixed. It's the quiet remembrance that the same cosmic energy moving the stars also moves through us—guiding us toward something greater.

To truly understand this shift, we must recognize that transformation doesn't begin outside of us. It begins within. Just as the stars move in harmony, our personal growth is inseparable from humanity's collective evolution.

A Childhood Glimpse of the Infinite

When I was nine years old, my brother and I were snowmobiling in the field across from our home. It was one of those clear, crisp winter nights when the stars felt impossibly close, and the world was painted in a serene palette of white and black. As we zipped through the snow, something in the sky caught our attention. A bright and unidentifiable object seemed to move toward us, then back up and away into the vastness of the night.

I vividly remember my brother's voice breaking the silence: "I think that was a flying saucer!" Without missing a beat, my nine-year-old self responded, "Of course it is."

In that moment, I felt both incredibly small and profoundly connected—as if the vastness of the universe wasn't intimidating but inviting. There was no skepticism, only an innate knowing: Who are we to believe we're the only lifeforms in this vast universe? Even at that young age, I felt it—the deep interconnectedness of all things, and the quiet knowing that we are part of something far greater than ourselves.

Looking back, I see that moment not just as a childhood curiosity, but as a quiet preview of what many are beginning to witness now. Around the world, sightings of unexplainable phenomena are becoming more frequent—not because they've suddenly increased, but because we're becoming more conscious. The veil is thinning. As our awareness expands, so too does our ability to perceive what has always been here.

Channelers like Darryl Anka—who brings through the being known as Bashar—have even spoken of a likely first contact event occurring in late 2026 or early 2027. Bashar is known for rarely making future predictions, acknowledging that timelines are fluid and shaped by collective choices. But in this case, the trajectory is becoming so stable that it's now seen as probable.

Whether or not that timing proves literal, the energy is unmistakable: we are not alone, and we are awakening to that truth.

Pluto in Aquarius—Personal Power and Collective Progress

Pluto is a celestial force of profound change. It reveals what's hidden, dismantling illusions, and clearing the way for rebirth. Its entrance into Aquarius marks a shift from personal transformation to collective awakening. This is a time to let go of outdated systems, beliefs, and structures that have kept us divided.

Aquarius, the water bearer, is not about chaos—it's about progress and innovation. Its energy emphasizes individuality within the collective, showing us that embracing our unique gifts strengthens the whole. Together, Pluto and Aquarius call us to co-create a new paradigm rooted in unity, compassion, and shared responsibility.

Aquarius is a sign of contradictions: fiercely individualistic yet deeply connected to the collective. It reminds us that our personal growth is not separate from the world around us. Instead, it ripples outward, inspiring change and healing in others.

In this Aquarian era, technology and spirituality will intersect in transformative ways. Innovations in communication, energy, and science will push humanity forward—but only if we use them wisely, with the intention of serving the collective rather than perpetuating division.

From Awakening to Alignment

The journey of transformation often begins with a single spark—a moment of awakening, like seeing a flying saucer in the sky or realizing that the structures you've always accepted no longer align with your truth. These personal moments of clarity are not isolated; they're part of a larger wave of collective evolution.

When we embrace our own transformation, we contribute to the awakening of humanity as a whole. Each act of self-awareness, compassion, and authenticity adds to the collective shift. In this way, the Aquarian energy reminds us that our growth is not just for ourselves—it's for everyone.

The cosmos often mirrors these inner and outer journeys. Quasars, supernovas, and other celestial phenomena serve as reminders of the infinite possibilities within the universe. They symbolize the death of the old and the birth of the new—a process that is just as much about evolution as it is about unity.

Think of a supernova—a star's dramatic end—not as destruction, but as creation. Its remnants become the building blocks for new stars and planets, a cosmic reminder that endings are often beginnings in disguise. The same is true in our lives: the transitions we face, no matter how challenging, are invitations to become something greater.

The universe doesn't just speak through stars and galaxies—it also communicates in the quiet, personal ways that touch our daily lives.

Have you ever glanced at a clock and noticed the same number sequence appearing again and again? These are not coincidences. Known as Angel Numbers, these repeating patterns are believed to carry divine guidance—offering reassurance or a gentle nudge to pay attention.

Take 555, for example. It often appears during times of change, signaling transformation and freedom. It's the universe's way of saying, "Embrace the shift. What feels uncertain now is clearing the way for something greater." Like Pluto's call for evolution, these signs invite us to trust the process.

When you notice these synchronicities, I invite you to pause. Reflect. Ask: *What message is the universe offering me right now?* These subtle cues are part of an ongoing dialogue between your consciousness and the cosmos. The more you tune in, the more clearly you begin to hear the language of transformation.

Embodying the Shift

Navigating this Aquarian era asks us not just to awaken—but to embody. This is a time for both inner work and inspired action. A time to live the awakening, not just understand it. Here are some soul-aligned practices to support you in embodying the shift:

Self-Reflection
Regularly examine old patterns and beliefs that no longer serve you. Ask yourself: What am I ready to release? What am I being called to embrace? Trust that letting go creates space for transformation.

Connect and Contribute
Surround yourself with others who share your vision for unity and growth. Meditate on how your personal choices ripple outward. Imagine your actions sending waves of light into the world.

Embrace Innovation

Stay open to technologies and tools that enhance spiritual and collective development. Use them with discernment, always asking: *Does this bring us closer to connection, or farther from it?*

Surrender to Transformation

Let go of the need to control every outcome. Trust that the unfolding is sacred—even when it feels unfamiliar. Rebirth often requires releasing what once felt safe.

Expand Your Awareness

Give yourself permission to wonder. Dream. Explore the mysteries of the universe. Just as my younger self instinctively accepted the flying saucer in the sky, allow yourself to embrace the unknown with curiosity and awe.

Pluto in Aquarius is more than an astrological event—it's a cosmic invitation. A call to co-create a future rooted in unity, compassion, and shared purpose.

Unity consciousness doesn't ask us to abandon our individuality. It asks us to bring it forward—in service of the collective. Each of us is a thread in humanity's great tapestry. When woven together with intention, we create something stronger and more beautiful than we ever could alone.

And as we awaken to this, the universe begins to speak—not in words, but in whispers. An unexpected encounter. A repeating number. A dream that lingers long after waking. These aren't accidents. They're invitations.

Each synchronicity is a spark. Each sign is a conversation. And every moment of awareness draws us closer to a life aligned with our soul's truth.

The cosmos is speaking. All we have to do is listen.

In the next chapter, we'll explore how to recognize these cosmic signs—not just as passing curiosities, but as meaningful messages. Synchronicity is the language of the universe, and when we learn to listen closely, we begin to walk in harmony with something far greater than ourselves.

The Language of the Universe—Synchronicity and Signs

"The universe is always speaking. Its language is not of words but of patterns, symbols, and subtle whispers. To listen is to awaken."

The whisper of synchronicity is subtle but unmistakable.

Have you ever experienced a coincidence so striking it felt as though the universe had orchestrated it just for you? Perhaps you thought of an old friend, only for them to call moments later. Or you kept seeing the same number sequence everywhere you looked. These moments aren't random. They are synchronicities—the universe's way of communicating, guiding, and nudging us toward alignment with our higher purpose.

These moments of connection often feel both comforting and uncanny, as if the unseen forces around us are offering a gentle nudge. They are not limited by time or space but seem to occur in perfect alignment with our emotional or spiritual needs.

Synchronicity is the language of the divine. It transcends logic, weaving through our lives as a subtle yet powerful reminder that we are part of something much greater. These signs often come when we need them most, reassuring us that we are on the right path or encouraging us to shift. But to truly hear the universe, we must learn to listen.

Numbers—Sacred Symbols of the Universe

I remember a time when the universe left me a trail of breadcrumbs in the form of repeating numbers. I was at a crossroads, wrestling with a life-changing decision. After years in the environmental field, I felt an undeniable pull to leave it all behind—not just switch jobs, but step away entirely to follow my dream of becoming an entrepreneur. It was terrifying, and I couldn't see how it would all come together.

That's when 444 began to appear everywhere—on receipts, clocks, and even license plates. At first, I dismissed it as a coincidence, but the repetition was too striking to ignore. Each time I saw it, I felt a quiet reassurance, like the universe whispered, *"Trust the process. You're supported."*

Later, I learned that 444 is often seen as an angel number—a divine message of protection, guidance, and encouragement to stay the course. That discovery only deepened what I already felt in my bones: I wasn't alone.

Following that feeling wasn't easy, but it gave me the courage to take the leap. Looking back, I can see how that decision shaped my life in ways I couldn't have imagined. What struck me most was how consistently the signs appeared—always emerging when doubt or fear crept in. They felt like planted markers, gently reminding me to pause, breathe, and trust. Over time, I came to see these numbers not just as signs but as tools to recalibrate my energy and realign with my purpose.

Among the many signs the universe offers, numbers hold a special place. Throughout history, numbers have been recognized as carriers of spiritual meaning. From Pythagoras to sacred geometry, they are seen as the building blocks of the cosmos, reflecting its order and harmony.

Take, for example, angel numbers like 111 or 555, which many people interpret as messages of new beginnings or transformation. But some numbers carry an even deeper resonance—acting as codes for awakening and connection to higher consciousness.

And one of the most powerful among them is 144—a number that carries its own sacred frequency.

The 144—Awakening the Code of Unity

The number 144 is not merely a number; it is an awakening code embedded within the fabric of existence. It corresponds to the *Circle of Life* and the *Flower of Life* pattern, where sacred geometry illustrates the interconnectedness of all things. Within this framework, 144 represents the fragmented aspects of self—the 144,000 expressions of our soul's essence spread across lifetimes, dimensions, and experiences. These are not literal parts to be counted, but symbolic of the vastness of who we are. Each piece holds wisdom, memory, and purpose—waiting to be remembered, reintegrated, and made whole.

This number carries a resonance that speaks to the soul, urging us to step beyond the mundane and into the extraordinary. Have you ever felt a sense of connection to something greater, even if you couldn't explain it? This is the energy of 144—a call to remember that life's complexities are not random but part of a divine design. It's a reminder that even the challenges we face serve a purpose, guiding us to a deeper understanding of our wholeness.

This code is a catalyst—awakening dormant energies, aligning us with higher consciousness, and inviting us to remember our wholeness. The 144 in you symbolizes the unification of these fragmented aspects, a call to reclaim the parts of yourself you once perceived as separate. What parts of yourself have you ignored, silenced, or hidden? What if those pieces hold the key to your fullest potential? It's an invitation to step into your multidimensional nature and recognize that every piece, no matter how fractured, is integral to your divine essence.

Imagine the *Flower of Life*, a sacred geometric pattern composed of overlapping circles. Each circle represents an aspect of the self, and together, they form a complete, harmonious whole. The 144 mirrors this pattern, reminding us that spiritual awakening involves integrating all aspects of being. This means honoring every piece of your story—the joys, the struggles, and the lessons—as part of a greater whole. This process often requires healing, forgiveness, and alignment with universal truths, but in doing so, we rediscover our divine potential.

By embracing the 144, we transcend the illusion of separation. We remember that we are already whole, divinely complete, and connected to the cosmic *Circle of Life*. For me, recognizing this unity helped me see the interconnectedness of my decisions and how they fit into a larger tapestry of purpose. It showed me that the choices I once questioned were, in fact, aligned with something greater—proof that the universe was always guiding me, even when I couldn't see the full picture.

As you reflect on the 144, consider this: What would life look like if you saw yourself as already whole, divinely complete, and infinitely connected to the universe? How might that belief change the way you approach your decisions, relationships, and sense of purpose?

Reading the Signs

Beyond numbers, the universe speaks through symbols, patterns, and everyday moments. Feathers, rainbows, recurring animals, or unexpected delays can all carry messages—offering guidance, reassurance, or the encouragement to pause and pay attention. These signs often align with our inner thoughts or emotions, creating a sense of synchronicity that goes beyond chance.

A repeating song lyric. A stranger's kind word. A traffic jam that reroutes your day and opens a new door. These aren't just coincidences. They're moments of meaning. The universe is always communicating—inviting you into an ongoing, living conversation.

The more you notice, the more the dialogue deepens. Sometimes, the messages are crystal clear. Other times, they're invitations to sit with curiosity, trusting that their meaning will unfold in divine timing.

To recognize these signs, you don't need to be psychic—just present, open, and willing to listen. The more grounded you are in the moment, the more attuned you become to the whispers the universe is offering.

Let's explore a few simple ways to begin noticing—and trusting—the signs around you.

Pay Attention: Start noticing patterns in your daily life. Are there recurring themes, symbols, or numbers? Write them down.

Trust Your Intuition: If something feels meaningful, it likely is. Intuition is your inner compass, guiding you to the significance of these signs.

Reflect on Timing: Synchronicities often occur when you're contemplating a decision or seeking clarity. Consider how the sign relates to what's happening in your life.

Ask for Guidance: Don't be afraid to ask the universe for a sign. Be specific and open to how it may appear.

Stay Present: The more you practice mindfulness, the more attuned you become to the subtle ways the universe communicates.

Living in Dialogue with the Divine

To live in harmony with the language of the universe is to embrace a life of trust, reverence, and co-creation. Synchronicities are not just signs to observe—they are invitations to deepen your relationship with the divine.

Here are a few practices to help integrate this sacred dialogue into your daily life:

Gratitude

Acknowledge the signs you receive. Say thank you aloud or in your heart. This strengthens your connection and encourages more guidance to come through.

Meditation

Spend time in stillness. The more you quiet the noise, the more clearly you'll hear the messages beneath it.

Alignment

Use synchronicities as energetic checkpoints. If something feels "off," pause. If a sign repeats, ask what it's confirming or redirecting.

Storytelling

Share your experiences with others. The more we speak about synchronicity, the more we normalize it. We amplify its presence by giving it a voice.

And sometimes, synchronicities do more than guide—they **connect**.

They reveal the invisible threads that weave our lives together. A chance encounter becomes a soul agreement. A painful relationship becomes a mirror for growth. A teacher shows up when you didn't even know you were ready to learn.

These are not random. These are the sacred bonds our souls may have agreed to long before this lifetime. Bonds that stretch across time, across dimensions, carrying purpose, activation, and evolution.

What if the person who frustrated you most was also your greatest teacher? What if the friend who appeared at just the right time was part of a divine contract—one written in stars, not ink?

When we honor these bonds, even the difficult ones, we begin to understand that life is not happening *to* us, but *with* us. That we are not alone, not broken, not wandering without meaning.

We are connected. Chosen. And divinely supported every step of the way.

As we begin to listen more closely to the universe's messages, something beautiful happens—we also start to recognize the people in our lives as part of that conversation. Every encounter, every soul connection, carries meaning.

In the next chapter, we'll explore the sacred bonds that shape our path. These relationships—whether fleeting or lifelong, challenging or cherished—are threads in the divine tapestry of your soul's evolution.

The Tapestry of Souls— Understanding Sacred Bonds

"Sacred bonds are the threads of our spiritual tapestry, and when a thread no longer serves, releasing it with love creates room for a masterpiece to emerge."

There are invisible threads that seem to weave through our lives— threads of destiny, connection, and purpose.

Have you ever met someone and felt an instant, inexplicable connection, as if they had been a part of your story long before your paths crossed? Maybe it was a friend who understood you like no one else, or someone who challenged you so deeply that it left an indelible mark on your soul. These encounters often defy logic yet feel profoundly significant. It's as though the universe has orchestrated these meetings to nudge us toward growth, healing, or understanding. When we pause to reflect, we realize that these connections, while rare, serve as signposts on our spiritual journey. These are no random encounters—they are sacred bonds, the threads that weave our lives together. Often called soul contracts, these are the agreements we forge long before we arrive on this earth.

Sacred bonds are the invisible threads weaving through the tapestry of our lives—guiding us to the lessons we need, and the love we are meant to give and receive. When we begin to see our relationships—both joyful and painful—as purposeful, our lives take on new meaning.

Let's explore the sacred nature of these connections and, just as importantly, how we can honor or release them when their purpose has been fulfilled. By the end of this chapter, you'll see how understanding these bonds can heal your heart, clarify your relationships, and lead you closer to the truth of who you are.

What Are Sacred Bonds?

Think of sacred bonds as spiritual blueprints, agreements you made with other souls before this life began. Imagine flipping through a book of possibilities, each page detailing lessons of courage, forgiveness, or resilience. These bonds are not meant to bind us but to guide us, revealing the path we're meant to walk. They serve as a compass, aligning us with the experiences our soul seeks.

Imagine gathering with those closest to you in a celestial workshop, sketching out your life's lessons, challenges, and joys. "You'll help me learn resilience," you might have said to one soul, while agreeing to teach another about forgiveness. These bonds are rooted in love, even when they seem anything but loving in the moment.

Each bond carries an energetic frequency, uniquely attuned to the lessons it's meant to bring. Think of these frequencies as vibrations—subtle signals that resonate with specific emotions or challenges.

Some bonds feel uplifting and warm, a reflection of love's ease and grace. Others feel heavier—draining at times, yet profoundly transformative. Both serve a purpose. Some connections feel like harmony—effortless and joyful. Others create contrast, stirring something within us that leads to discomfort and growth.

Harmony nurtures our spirit. Contrast challenges it. But it's often through the challenging bonds that we're invited to confront aspects of ourselves we might otherwise overlook.

Sacred bonds often manifest in relationships that feel intense, deeply familiar, or transformative. Not every connection is a sacred bond, but the ones that are tend to leave a lasting imprint.

These might include:

- The family you're born into, shaping your early beliefs and patterns.
- A romantic partner who teaches you about vulnerability, trust, or self-worth.
- A friend who supports you through life's storms and reminds you of your strength.
- Even an adversary who challenges you to stand in your power.

But here's the truth: sacred bonds are not prisons. They are living, breathing agreements that evolve as you do. When the lessons are learned or the growth has occurred, some bonds can and should be released. This release is not an abandonment but a recognition of completion—a way to honor the journey while allowing space for new connections and growth. By understanding this process, we begin to see release not as loss but as liberation, paving the way for deeper alignment with our soul's path.

The Purpose Behind the Pain

It's not always easy to recognize the purpose of a sacred bond when you're in the thick of it. The pain can feel consuming, blinding us to the gifts hidden within it. Yet, it is often through discomfort that the soul grows. The relationships that challenge us the most are often the ones that push us toward our greatest evolution. Painful relationships can feel more like punishment than purpose. But let me share a deeply personal story—my own.

My husband, Al, and I have been married for many years. He is one of the most loving, honest, and steadfast people I know—but we are also very different in how we see the world, handle emotions, and communicate. At times, those differences have clashed, leaving me frustrated, misunderstood, or overwhelmed. And through the years, Al has managed—often unknowingly—to push nearly every button I have.

There were moments when I questioned why it had to be so hard. But as the years unfolded, I began to see something beautiful beneath the surface of our struggles. Al wasn't my adversary; he was my greatest teacher.

The moments of struggle were like mirrors, reflecting back not just his actions but my reactions. I began to ask myself: Why does this hurt? Why does this frustrate me? These questions unearthed wounds I hadn't even realized I was carrying—childhood insecurities, unspoken fears, and unresolved grief.

Al wasn't just pushing my buttons; he was illuminating the areas within me that needed attention. His steadfast approach challenged me to slow down, listen deeply, and soften my reactive edges.

When I felt misunderstood, it nudged me to reflect on how well I understood myself. When our disagreements felt unbearable, they showed me where old wounds were still asking for healing.

It wasn't easy work. Sacred bonds rarely are. But as I began to shift my perspective, I saw our marriage in a new light. Instead of seeing the conflict as something to fix, I saw it as an opportunity to grow. I realized that Al's role in my life wasn't just as my partner; he was a mirror reflecting back to me the areas where I needed to evolve.

When we embrace the deeper purpose of our relationships, something powerful happens. This doesn't mean we excuse bad behavior or ignore our own needs. Instead, it invites us to see challenges as stepping stones to greater self-awareness.

For me, the growth that came from our sacred bond strengthened not just our marriage but my own sense of self. Al taught me patience, resilience, and how to love more fully—not just him, but myself.

This is the beauty of sacred bonds. Even in pain, they guide us toward healing and self-discovery. They remind us that nothing is wasted—not the heartbreak, the conflict, or the tears. When we see our relationships through this lens of purpose, we create space for transformation, connection, and, most importantly, love.

Recognizing and Releasing Your Sacred Bonds

How do you know if a relationship is a sacred bond? Sometimes it's the immediate connection—as if you've known this person far longer than this lifetime. Other times, it's the emotional charge the relationship carries: love, grief, anger, joy, or all of the above. Sacred bonds tend to leave an imprint. They linger in your heart, your memory, or your energy long after the moment has passed.

Here are a few signs to help you recognize one:

- You feel an instant and powerful connection, as if you've known the person forever.
- The relationship stirs deep emotions—love, anger, grief, or all of them at once.
- You notice patterns repeating, pointing to lessons you're meant to learn.
- The bond feels transformative, leaving you changed in ways you can't fully explain.

But what happens when the bond has served its purpose?

Releasing a sacred bond is not abandonment. It's acknowledgment. It's a loving act of closure for what was—a conscious choice to evolve beyond its original form. The release doesn't make the relationship less sacred—it honors its completion.

And while this kind of letting go is rarely easy, it becomes more graceful when we approach it with intention and care. One way to do that is through a heart-centered process for release.

Here are a few simple, soul-honoring steps to support that process:

1. Acknowledge the Bond
Reflect on what the relationship taught you. Was it trust? Boundaries? Self-love? Honor the lessons, even if they came wrapped in challenges.

2. Seek Closure
If possible, have an honest conversation. If not, write a letter you don't send, or create a personal ritual that brings symbolic completion.

3. Set an Intention
Visualize the energetic tie between you and the other person. Imagine it gently dissolving in light and love. Affirm that you release them—and yourself—with peace.

4. Trust the Process
Releasing doesn't erase the impact. It simply opens space for what's next. Completion is not a loss—it's an expansion.

Letting go isn't a rejection. It's a rite of passage.

Think of it as a soul graduation—where the chapter ends, but the wisdom remains. The relationship may no longer live in your daily life, but its imprint lives on in who you've become.

Embracing the Tapestry—Past, Present, and the Path Forward

Every sacred bond, whether it brought joy or challenge, belongs to the divine choreography of your life. Some arrive to stay. Some arrive to shift you. Some arrive only to show you a part of yourself you forgot to love. Each one plays a part in the evolution of your soul.

When we honor the full spectrum of connection—without clinging or judging—we align with the deeper rhythm of life. This is the divine dance. A waltz of presence, release, and remembrance. Even the most painful relationships hold a kind of sacred beauty when viewed through the lens of growth.

And when we release what no longer serves, we don't lose the love—we expand its capacity.

As we open our hearts to healing, we begin to see our story as part of something greater. The threads of our sacred bonds are not limited to this lifetime—they echo through generations. The joys, wounds, and patterns we carry are often not ours alone. They are the whispers of our ancestors, the soul agreements we inherited, and the opportunities we now hold to transform them.

Every pattern we heal, every bond we release with love, becomes a ripple of freedom for those who came before us—and those yet to come.

When we honor the strength of our lineage, we reclaim what's good and allow what's outdated to dissolve. Healing becomes a legacy. A quiet revolution. A way to plant seeds of compassion, clarity, and liberation for future generations.

So ask yourself:

- What echoes from the past are still shaping your choices today?
- What sacred bonds are you ready to honor, forgive, or release?
- What future are you weaving, thread by conscious thread?

These echoes don't just call us to look back—they invite us to transform pain into wisdom and challenges into blessings.

The tapestry is never finished. But each time you choose love, you strengthen the pattern.

Each sacred bond you understand, each soul agreement you release, becomes a doorway—leading you further into the truth of who you are.

As we move forward, we'll explore how the whispers of time carry the seeds of transformation—shaping not only our personal growth, but the collective healing of all who walk this path.

Whispers Through Time— Transforming Generational Wounds into Wisdom

"Through the sacred act of healing, we become the bridge between the wisdom of the past and the promise of the future."

The voices that whisper through time don't always shout—they arrive as patterns, instincts, or familiar phrases we didn't know we'd memorized.

Have you ever paused to wonder if your struggles are entirely your own? What if the patterns you face echo the lives of those who came before you? The idea is both humbling and empowering: we are more connected to our lineage than we often realize, and within this connection lies profound potential for healing and transformation.

Have you ever noticed a pattern in your life and thought, Why does this keep happening to me? Maybe it's a cycle of relationships that seem to end the same way or an internal battle you can't quite shake. Now, imagine this: what if these struggles weren't entirely your own? What if they carried the echoes of those who came before you—your parents, grandparents, and ancestors stretching back through time?

It's a humbling thought, isn't it? That the pain, the joy, the choices, and even the silence of our ancestors ripple through us, shaping the lives we lead today.

I first began to notice this in my own life when I would catch myself saying, 'Finish what's on your plate,' and I heard my grandmother's voice coming out of my mouth. Noni, being the quintessential Italian grandma, loved to feed us. She'd say, 'Mangia!' with such joy, insisting we clean our plates and often pushing for seconds. But I suspected it was more than just her love of feeding us. Beneath her words lingered something deeper—a cellular memory of scarcity left over from the Great Depression, when food was precious, and every meal felt like a gift.

I understood why she'd said it, but I also realized I wasn't just repeating her words—I was channeling her fear of scarcity, even though my circumstances were so different. In that moment, I realized I wasn't just living my story—I was living *our* story. A lineage of choices and circumstances handed down through generations. This realization was both humbling and empowering. It made me question how much of my life I had been living unconsciously, following patterns that weren't truly mine. Each time I caught myself repeating a behavior or belief, I began to wonder: *Is this really me, or is this a reflection of my ancestors?* That question became a key to understanding not only my struggles but also my potential to break free.

But here's the beautiful part: when we recognize these patterns, we have the power to heal them—not just for ourselves, but for those who came before us and those yet to come.

Let's take a closer look at these ancestral echoes: how they shape us, how they wound us, and how we can turn those wounds into wisdom.

The Influence of Ancestral Patterns

Picture this: a river flowing through time, carrying everything in its path—pebbles, twigs, even boulders. Some of it is beautiful, like the glistening water and sunlight dancing on the surface. But some of it is heavy, murky, and stagnant. This is the river of inheritance that flows through each of us.

Our ancestors leave us more than just our eye color or the shape of our smile. They pass down the stories of their lives: the dreams they dared to pursue, the fears they couldn't escape, and the wounds they never quite healed. These imprints are carried in our behaviors, beliefs, and sometimes even our bodies.

Take, for example, the idea of scarcity. Maybe you grew up in a family where money was tight, and the phrase "We can't afford that" became a mantra. Even as you achieve success, you might feel a persistent fear of losing it all, as if scarcity is your default setting. That fear may not be yours alone; it might be an echo of a time when your ancestors struggled to put food on the table.

Even if you grew up in a world of abundance, that fear of scarcity might linger like a shadow, influencing decisions, relationships, and self-worth. This isn't about blaming our ancestors—it's about recognizing the threads they've woven into our lives. With recognition comes the power to choose differently.

Science even backs this up. Researchers studying epigenetics have found that trauma can leave marks on our DNA, altering how genes are expressed. In essence, the effects of a painful event—war, famine, displacement—can be passed down through generations, even if the original wound wasn't yours to bear.

For instance, studies on Holocaust survivors and their descendants have shown genetic markers that suggest inherited trauma, offering concrete evidence of this profound connection.

But trauma isn't all we inherit. Courage, creativity, and wisdom are just as deeply woven into our DNA. The same genetic markers that carry pain also carry the potential for resilience and transformation.

Recognizing this duality allows us to honor both the wounds and the strengths of our lineage—and it gives us the power to begin healing what our ancestors couldn't.

Breaking Cycles, Healing Generations

Here's the empowering truth: we are not bound by the patterns we inherit. While our ancestors may have handed us a script, we hold the pen. We can write a new story.

The first step in breaking a cycle is recognizing it. For me, this began with asking hard questions: What patterns have repeated in my family? What unspoken rules or fears have I absorbed without realizing it? I invite you to do the same. Reflect on your family's dynamics and ask yourself where the same themes show up in your own life. This reflection doesn't just shine a light on the wounds—it also reveals the gifts. By tracing your family's stories, you might uncover hidden strengths: a grandmother's unshakable determination, a father's quiet acts of kindness, or an ancestor's ability to find joy in the simplest things. These are the treasures woven into the fabric of who you are.

Once you've identified a pattern, the next step is compassion. It's easy to feel frustrated with those who came before us, especially when their actions or choices created pain. But here's the thing: our ancestors were human, just like us. They were doing the best they could with the tools they had at the time. When we approach their stories with compassion, we free ourselves from resentment and open the door to healing.

One of the most powerful ways I've found to heal generational wounds is through ritual. For me, this has included journaling letters to my ancestors, thanking them for their sacrifices and acknowledging the wounds they carried. Sometimes, I'll light a candle as I reflect, imagining its flame as a beacon of light traveling back through time, offering love and peace to those who came before me.

Another tool is setting boundaries—not just with people in the present but with the patterns of the past. Just because a belief or behavior was handed down to you doesn't mean you have to carry it forward.

By breaking free from these cycles, you're not rejecting your ancestors—you're honoring them. You're walking a path of healing they may not have had the chance to walk.

And sometimes, that healing arrives unexpectedly.

During my editing process, as I read this chapter aloud to feel the rhythm and cadence of its words, I had one of those moments. A spontaneous wave of energy surged through me as my voice began to shift. Toning, hand movements, and *Light Language* flowed through me in a way that felt completely natural—yet undeniably sacred.

You may not be familiar with the term *Light Language*—we'll explore it in a later chapter—but it's a form of energetic expression that bypasses the logical mind and speaks directly to the soul.

Though I hadn't planned it, I knew exactly what was happening: I wasn't just speaking about ancestral healing—I was conducting it.

I'll share more about that experience later, but I offer it now as a reminder:

This work is not conceptual. It's alive. When you say yes to healing your lineage, your body, voice, and spirit will respond in ways that are deeply intelligent—even if you don't yet have words for what's unfolding.

The Gifts of Our Lineage

As much as we discuss the wounds of the past, it's equally important to honor the gifts. Our ancestors may have struggled, but they also triumphed. They loved, created, and dreamed, and those blessings live on in us, too.

I think of my own lineage and the strength of the women who came before me. Their courage in the face of hardship, their creativity, and their deep connection to nature are threads I see woven into my own life.

Sometimes, the gifts of our ancestors show up in unexpected ways. Consider how these gifts might manifest in your daily life. Perhaps you've inherited your grandmother's green thumb, finding solace in tending to plants, or your grandfather's knack for storytelling, captivating others with your words. These inherited talents aren't just hobbies—they're echoes of the love and passion your ancestors carried.

This became clear to me when I rediscovered a painting I'd created decades ago—a watercolor of a purple twilight sky and ocean, with six dolphins leaping in the air. I had tucked it away in the attic and forgotten about it until recently. When I found it, I felt an instant connection. It felt familiar yet otherworldly, as if it carried a deeper meaning I couldn't quite put into words.

After framing it for my office, I began to see it differently. It wasn't just a painting; it was a symbol of something larger. In a recent spiritual reading, I learned of my connection to Sirius B and C, and suddenly, the dolphins in the painting made sense. They were more than animals; they were guides, representing joy, freedom, and a bridge between earthly and cosmic wisdom.

This experience reminded me that our lineage isn't just earthly—it's cosmic too. We are connected not only to those who walked this earth before us but to the stars and beyond.

Embracing the Sacred Thread— Healing Across Time

Healing generational wounds isn't about erasing the past—it's about transforming it. When we choose to break cycles and honor the gifts of our lineage, we create ripples of healing that reach backward and forward through time.

When I think about my dolphin painting, I see it as a metaphor for this journey. It reminds me that our ancestors are not just behind us—they are within us, guiding us with their whispers, wisdom, and dreams.

When we embrace this perspective, we step into a space where healing becomes possible, not just for ourselves but also for future generations. This is how we honor the past and create a future of love, freedom, and connection.

As we heal the echoes of our ancestors, we begin to see that our journey is not just about breaking cycles—it is about weaving a new story, one that honors the past while embracing the infinite potential of the present. Through this healing, the fragments of pain and wisdom merge, revealing a deeper truth: we are not just shaped by those who came before us—we are guided by something greater.

Healing generational wounds isn't the end of the story—it's the beginning of a deeper journey. When we honor the past and heal the future, we step into a sacred space where time feels fluid, and connection transcends generations. It's as though the voices of our ancestors, once filled with pain, transform into whispers of encouragement, guiding us toward the light.

The path ahead invites us into something even deeper—into the space where spirit meets mystery. Part 4, *Integration and Mysticism*, opens a new doorway. It is here, in the space between the seen and unseen, that we begin to remember the light we've been carrying all along—a divine spark, quietly waiting to be awakened.

What if that spark is the bridge between humanity and the infinite?

PART 4
Integration and Mysticism

"Mysticism is not about knowing all the answers, it's about trusting the questions. Integration comes when we learn to dance with the mystery and let its whispers lead us home."

The Christ Within—Remembering Your Divine Spark

"The second coming of Christ isn't an arrival; it's an awakening. The Christ you seek is already within you, waiting to be remembered."

There are moments in life so profound they etch themselves into your soul—becoming memories you return to again and again. One of those moments came for me on a rainy night aboard a tall ship, sailing from New Haven Harbor to Newport, Rhode Island, when the ocean came alive with bioluminescence.

During my years in the environmental field, I was part of a cooperative working to revitalize the harbor—bringing life and activity back to its waters. One of our initiatives was sponsoring tall ship cruises—a chance for people to experience the beauty of the harbor firsthand. While the tall ship cruise felt like a leisure outing, it was technically a working vessel—and every passenger had to sign up for a chore.

To everyone's surprise, I chose the night watch. Most people assumed I'd gravitate toward the galley because of my love for cooking, but I had a different pull. I wanted to be under the stars, enveloped by the quiet stillness of the night, where the world felt vast and infinite.

The professional crew set the sails in a way that acted as a natural anchor, keeping us in place. My job was simple but important: keep an eye out for other boats and ensure we didn't drift into the shipping lanes. I had imagined a clear night sky, with stars so bright they seemed to sing. But the universe had other plans.

Instead of the starlit night I had envisioned, the heavens opened with a steady rain, obscuring the stars behind a dense curtain of clouds. I could have given in to disappointment, but something told me to stay open, to remain curious about what this moment might offer.

I donned my raingear and walked the deck, listening to the gentle rhythm of the waves against the hull. I paused by the rail. Then I saw it.

Below me, the water came alive with light. Bioluminescence danced with every gentle wave, like a million tiny stars scattered across the ocean's surface.

I stood there, mesmerized. The phrase "as above, so below" echoed in my mind. In that moment, I understood something profound: the divine isn't confined to the heavens. It is everywhere—in the stars, in the ocean, and within each of us. Gaia herself carries this light, reflecting the cosmos back to us. The bioluminescence wasn't just a phenomenon; it was a mirror, reminding me that this same light exists within all of us, waiting to be seen.

A Mirror in the Water— Seeing the Divine Spark

This experience stayed with me—not just as a magical memory, but as a revelation. The light I saw in the water wasn't separate from the light in the sky, just as the divine spark within us isn't separate from the greater divine.

It's easy to forget this in the noise of daily life. We search for meaning in achievements, relationships, or spiritual leaders, believing salvation lies somewhere outside ourselves. Yet the most profound answers often live in stillness, quietly waiting to be remembered.

That spark within you is not new. It's ancient, eternal—and already alive inside you.

We've been conditioned to look outward for guidance, as though truth only lives in others. But what if the second coming of Christ isn't an external event at all? What if it's an internal awakening happening one soul at a time?

Imagine a seed buried deep in the soil. It doesn't awaken because of some force outside itself. It stirs from within, answering a quiet call. You are that seed. And the Christing is your awakening.

I believe Yeshua—known to many as Jesus—walked this Earth, embodying divine love in human form. His presence was real, powerful, and transformative. But the Christ wasn't limited to one man or one time in history. What if *Christ* also represents a state of divine consciousness—a way of being rooted in unconditional love, unity, and divine wisdom?

In some spiritual traditions, the word *Christing* has emerged to describe the sacred process of awakening the divine essence within.

The Christing, then, is not about becoming someone else—it's the remembrance of what's always lived inside you. It's a return to who you truly are.

This inner light isn't reserved for saints or mystics. It's available to anyone willing to open their heart. Regardless of spiritual background or belief, this invitation transcends dogma. It is a call to awaken your own divine essence.

Remembering the Light—Trusting the Sacred Unfolding

If the Christ within is always present, why is it so often forgotten?

Life surrounds us with noise. Cultural expectations tell us our worth is measured by what we produce, who we impress, or how much we achieve. These distractions keep us looking outward, never inward.

We begin to believe the light within us has dimmed—when in truth, it's only been veiled.

Some of the most common blocks to awakening include:

- **Cultural Noise:** The world constantly tells us to chase validation, productivity, or perfection. However, none of those things truly define our essence.
- **Fear and Doubt:** Many of us fear our own power. We question whether we're worthy of divine love, and in doing so, we shrink ourselves.
- **Egoic Illusions:** The ego loves to whisper that we are alone, separate, or lacking. But those whispers are just echoes of old programming—not truth.

These obstacles act like fog on the soul's mirror. They obscure, but they cannot extinguish what's real. Your light is like a lighthouse in the storm—steady, unwavering, and always guiding you home.

So how do we return to that light?

Here are a few gentle ways to reconnect with your inner divinity:

Silence the Noise: Create sacred moments of silence in your day. Whether through meditation, journaling, or a quiet walk in nature, stillness creates space for the soul's whisper to rise.

Practice Love: Start with yourself. Soften toward the parts of you that feel unworthy. Treat them not as flaws but as younger versions of you asking to be seen.

Live in Unity: See others not as separate, but as reflections of the same divine spark. When you serve others with love, you nourish the Christ within you.

Trust the Process: Awakening isn't linear. Some days will feel radiant, while others will feel uncertain. Trust that every step—even the messy ones—is part of your unfolding.

These are not rules or rituals to perfect. They are invitations to return.

The path to awakening doesn't ask you to strive or stretch. It asks you to remember. To rest in the knowing that the divine has never left you—it has only been waiting to be seen.

Becoming the Light—Embodying, Remembering, and Receiving

When you awaken to the Christ within, your light begins to shine. And here's the beautiful part: your light doesn't just transform your own life—it creates a ripple that touches others.

By embracing your divine spark, you invite others to embrace theirs. Your presence becomes a mirror, reflecting what's possible when we live in alignment with love, unity, and soul.

In a world that often feels divided or chaotic, your light becomes an anchor. Not just for you, but for those around you. It reminds others that peace is possible—not as a distant dream, but as a lived reality.

The Christing isn't about becoming someone else. It's about finally becoming yourself.

When you peel back the layers of fear and doubt, you find the light that's been there all along. That light doesn't just guide you—it illuminates the path for others. This is how we rise together. This is how awakening becomes collective.

This is the invitation of awakening: to no longer seek the light, but to recognize that you are it. Take a moment today to sit quietly and say to yourself, *"I am the light, and the light is me."*

Awakening the Christ within transforms how you see and experience the world. No longer limited to what your senses can perceive, you begin to tune in to something deeper—a universal frequency that resonates with your soul.

The divine often speaks in ways beyond words.
Through symbols etched in light, vibrations that echo in your heart, and a language as ancient as the stars, the universe offers a sacred conversation. You are not separate from it—you are part of it.

This inner awakening isn't just an experience.
It's a remembering.
It's a communion.
It's a return to the language of divine light—the resonance that has always been within you, guiding you home.

Let us step forward into this mystery—where light itself becomes the messenger, carrying the wisdom of the infinite and unlocking the divine spark within.

The Language of Light— A Gateway to the Divine

Light language isn't something you learn; it's a remembrance of your soul's infinite song.

This inward journey isn't just about finding peace; it's about uncovering the divine connection that has always been within you. Light language is one way we remember this connection. It is a sacred tool that speaks directly to the soul, bypassing the mind and awakening the light we all carry.

A New Voice Emerges

Have you ever felt something move through you—something inexplicable yet profound? A voice that wasn't yours yet felt familiar?

For many, the first encounter with light language feels like discovering a long-lost part of themselves. It's not a skill to be mastered but a resonance to be felt. The body might respond with subtle movements, vibrations, or sensations that defy explanation, leaving us in awe of the divine intelligence at work.

For me, it started subtly: an odd twitch in my left hand while I meditated, my fingers moving faster than I could consciously control. It looked like sign language—but more. As if my body were speaking a forgotten dialect that my mind hadn't yet learned to interpret.

Then came the sounds—beautiful, melodic notes that stunned me. I couldn't sing to save my life, yet what flowed from my lips felt pure, otherworldly. As the weeks passed, these notes evolved into words—syllables and tones I had never heard before. I was in awe, not afraid.

A few months later, I discovered what it was: light language.

If you've never heard of light language before, you're not alone. Yet, for many of us, it's a gift waiting patiently to be remembered. Light language is not bound to earthly rules or definitions. It transcends the spoken word, carrying sound, light, energy, and sacred geometry to activate, heal, and transform us at the deepest levels of our being.

The Essence of Light Language— Vibrations, Codes, and Cosmic Connection

Light language doesn't ask to be understood—it asks to be felt. It's like hearing a melody so pure that it calls out to a part of you that's been asleep. Its power lies in its simplicity: it bypasses layers of conditioning and speaks directly to the essence of who you are.

Often described as source language, light language is a vibrational technology. It doesn't follow grammar or structure like spoken word. Instead, it flows through tones, symbols, and frequencies—delivered through singing, chanting, movement, or hand gestures.

Imagine light language as the music of the universe. Each sound or movement carries cosmic information—energy designed to recalibrate your field. Just as you would tune an instrument to perfect pitch, light language tunes you to your highest frequency.

Many guides describe it as spiritual technology—a bridge between our human experience and divine consciousness. It offers a vibrational template that aligns us with higher states of being.

This is where *galactic light codes* come in. Many who channel light language experience these transmissions as messages from compassionate star beings—energetic imprints that carry wisdom from realms beyond Earth. These beings have walked similar paths and don't arrive as saviors, but as mentors—reminding us of what we already hold inside.

Their messages are invitations, not instructions. They invite us to remember our power, to expand our awareness, and to co-create with the universe from a place of soul.

Rather than fixing us, these codes resonate at a soul level—awakening memory, activating clarity, and stirring transformation. They speak in archetypal frequencies that bypass the logical mind and reach a deeper truth within.

When you hear or speak light language, you don't need to understand it with your intellect. Like a childhood lullaby, the message lives in the energy. You may not know the words, but the remembrance is unmistakable—something ancient inside you stirs.

These codes don't teach you—they *remind* you. Of who you've been, who you are, and who you're becoming.

Trusting the Unknown—My Light Language Journey and Its Purpose in This Time

When I first began channeling light language, I didn't know what to call it. My hands moved of their own accord, and beautiful sounds escaped my lips. At no point did I stop to question it. I was simply curious— fascinated by this experience that felt both strange and natural.

Curiosity became my anchor. I didn't resist or fear it; I allowed it to unfold. It felt like a dance with the universe—one where I didn't know the steps but trusted the rhythm.

At first, the movements and sounds were subtle—like whispers from the beyond. But as I surrendered, the energy grew stronger. It felt like a current flowing through me—a lifeline connecting me to something infinite. I realized I wasn't "making it up." I was simply allowing something greater to move through me.

And that's the essence of light language: it asks us to trust. To let go of the need for logic or control. To surrender to the mystery.

I also want to thank Aurora Luna Star, whose gentle encouragement helped me embrace verbal light language. While hand gestures and tonal expressions came naturally to me, speaking light language aloud felt like stepping into the unknown. Aurora's wisdom and support gave me the confidence to find my voice, unlocking a deeper connection to this sacred gift. Her guidance reminded me that we're never truly alone on this journey.

We are living in a time of great transformation. Our world is in flux, and with it comes the deep call to reconnect with something greater. Light language offers that bridge. It tunes us into the energetic shifts happening around and within us. It brings comfort in chaos—a vibrational balm that reminds us we are held.

Collectively, we're being asked to shed old patterns, heal ancestral wounds, and awaken to our true nature. And for many, that process feels overwhelming.

But light language offers an unexpected gift: a shortcut to alignment.

It works beneath the mind, touching the subtle layers of our being— places where words cannot reach. It soothes our energy field, dissolving blocks and limitations we didn't even know we carried.

When you hear or speak light language, it's like receiving an energetic upgrade—a transmission that says: *You are more than your fear. You are light. You are whole.*

Receiving the Frequency—How Light Language Speaks to the Soul and Guides Your Practice

Light language transcends logic. It invites us to feel, not think. It operates on a frequency that resonates with the heart rather than the mind—stirring emotions, memories, and a sense of ancient recognition that words cannot reach.

Imagine someone playing a note on a violin. You don't need to understand music theory to feel its vibration in your chest. Light language works the same way.

Each sound, tone, or gesture carries a frequency your soul recognizes. It's as though someone is pointing to a forgotten part of you and saying, *"Remember this. This is who you are."*

Whether you're channeling light language yourself or receiving it from others, the energy works on subtle levels. You might feel warmth, tingling, or a sense of lightness. You might feel nothing at all. Either way—something is happening beneath the surface.

Light language bypasses the filters of the thinking mind and speaks directly to your divine essence. It reminds you of your wholeness and helps clear away what no longer serves—making space for deeper alignment and expansion.

So how can you begin to engage with this sacred tool?

You don't need a method or mastery. You just need to be open.

Here are a few gentle ways to begin:

- **Allow Yourself to Receive**
  When you come across light language—whether in meditation, video, or a live session—simply receive it. Don't analyze or translate it. Let it wash over you and trust that energy knows what to do.

- **Trust What Comes Through**
  If you feel called to channel light language, trust it. It may start with a sound, a movement, or even scribbles on a page. Let it flow without judgment.

- **Notice Subtle Shifts**
  After experiencing light language, tune in. Do you feel lighter, more open, or deeply still? Maybe an old emotion rises to the surface. Honor it all. Your energy is responding.

- **Be Curious, Not Critical**
  Light language isn't meant to fit into a box. It defies logic. Approach it with wonder, like a sacred language from your soul you're just beginning to remember.

Remembering the Song— Surrendering to the Mystery

Light language is more than sounds or symbols—it's a homecoming. It reconnects us to the infinite wisdom within and around us. It's a reminder that we are not alone—that the universe is alive, conscious, and always speaking to us.

Perhaps you've felt the stirrings of light language yourself—a subtle movement, a sound, or a whisper you couldn't quite explain. I invite you to trust it. Allow yourself to become the vessel.

Just recently, while editing the chapter *Whispers Through Time: Transforming Generational Wounds into Wisdom*, I had an experience that can only be described as divinely orchestrated.

I was sitting at my desk, reading the section aloud—something I often do to feel the rhythm of my words—when suddenly, a wave of energy moved through me. Without warning, I began toning, speaking, and moving my hands in light language. The sounds, gestures, and frequencies were woven together in a way I had never experienced before—effortless, fluid, and deeply alive.

There was no translation, no English words, but somehow, I knew exactly what was being said.

It lasted for five or six minutes, and when it was over, I was overcome with emotion. Gratitude washed over me. I hadn't just written about ancestral healing—I had *become* the channel for it. I wasn't performing or interpreting; I was simply allowing it to move through me, trusting that something sacred was unfolding far beyond my understanding.

And that's what light language does—it bypasses the mind and opens the gateway for something greater to flow. In that moment, I believe I was conducting the very healing that the chapter was written to invite.

The language of light is not something to be learned; it's something to be remembered. And as you remember, you awaken to your divine nature—one note, one sound, one light code at a time.

Light language teaches us to surrender—to let go of control and trust the flow of divine energy.

Surrender doesn't mean giving up; it means leaning in. It's an act of courage to let the unknown lead, trusting that what lies ahead is not random but divinely orchestrated.

In every tone of light language—and in every moment of life's uncertainty—there's a quiet invitation:
You are not alone.
The journey is unfolding exactly as it should.

It's a dance in which we don't need to know the steps—we only need to follow the rhythm of our soul.

In much the same way, life invites us to embrace its mysteries. To lean into the unknown not with fear, but with curiosity. Not with resistance, but with reverence.

What if the mystery isn't something to solve, but an invitation to expand?

What if every unanswered question holds the key to a deeper transformation, leading us to doors we didn't even know existed?

Life, like light language, is a sacred act of trust.

And as we learn to surrender to its rhythm, something profound begins to emerge:
our own frequency—ready to be spoken, lived, and shared.

As we continue the journey inward, we begin to uncover something deeper—
not just a feeling or knowing, but a voice.

A frequency rising from the core of who we are.

One that doesn't echo old stories, but speaks with truth, resonance, and power.

In the next chapter, we'll explore how that voice becomes a sacred instrument—
not just for expression, but for awakening.

The Voice of Awakening—Truth, Frequency, and the Power of Words

"Your voice is not just sound—it's a vibration that reshapes reality."

In early March of 2025, I found myself glued to a conversation between Lee Harris and Emilio Ortiz on Just Tap In. Their words carried a frequency I could feel in my chest—not just thoughts, but transmission. They were speaking of global energy shifts, collective upgrades, and something that struck a deeper chord: a transformation happening within our voices.

Lee shared how he'd recently lost his voice while on tour—completely unable to speak. What began as a physical issue became, in his words, a "throat chakra upgrade." He described it not as a breakdown, but a reconfiguration—a lotus unfolding, energetically and literally. As he spoke, something inside me stirred. Not because I'd had the same experience, but because I knew the feeling he was pointing to: that sense of your voice no longer being just yours. Of it becoming something more. Something sacred.

That interview wasn't just an update—it was a reflection of something I had already begun noticing, both in myself and in my clients. A shift was happening. A deep re-tuning. Not in how we speak, but in what we carry *through* our words.

We are no longer being asked to say more.
We're being asked to say what's true.

The Energy Behind the Words

We've all been taught to use our voice—to speak up, speak clearly, speak confidently. But what we haven't always been taught is that what we speak carries energy, and that energy is often louder than the words themselves.

You can say all the "right" things and still create dissonance if the vibration behind your words is out of alignment.
You can whisper one sentence with love and shift the entire room.

In this season of awakening, we are being invited to listen more deeply—not just to others, but to ourselves.
To feel the resonance of our words before they leave our mouths.
To ask: Is what I'm about to say coming from fear… or from truth?

This isn't about being polished or perfect. It's about being energetically honest.

I've come to see voice not as a tool—but as a tuning fork. One that vibrates with our frequency in real time. And when that frequency shifts, our voice must shift too.

When Speaking Up Meant Standing Alone

I wasn't always this clear in my voice.

There were times I held back—not because I didn't know what I wanted to say, but because I feared what might happen if I said it. I've been in conversations where I felt the words rising in my throat but stopped them mid-breath, too afraid they'd be "too much" or "too different." I've also been in rooms where I spoke anyway, my voice shaking but steady, knowing that silence would've cost me more than discomfort.

In those moments, my voice wasn't just speaking—it was **remembering**. Remembering who I was before I learned to censor myself. Remembering the truth I carried long before I had the vocabulary to explain it.

I remember the first time I talked openly about being intuitive in a professional setting. My palms were sweating. I was sure people would think I was unqualified or unstable. But I said it anyway. "I know this might sound strange, but I work with energy. I listen to what isn't being said. I tune into the frequency behind your words."
And then came the silence.

But what followed next surprised me.

One woman leaned forward and said, "I've always felt things that way, too... I just never had the words for it."

That's when I realized: our truth activates other people's remembering.

Speaking Is an Act of Embodiment

Our voice is more than our words. It's the vibration of everything we've lived.
It's our heartbreaks, our healings, our shadows, our sovereignty.

Every time we speak with presence, we anchor a frequency into the field. And that frequency either perpetuates a story... or transforms it.

For those of us walking a spiritual path, this becomes even more crucial. The more aligned we become, the more responsibility we carry—not to be perfect, but to be intentional. To speak our truth—not just with conviction, but with compassion. Because words, once spoken, don't disappear. They echo. They ripple. They imprint.

Trusting the Truth That Wants to Be Spoken

There is a voice within you that already knows what needs to be said.

You may feel it as a whisper in your heart before you enter a conversation.
You may sense it rising when someone crosses a boundary.
Or you may hear it in the quiet moments—those subtle nudges that say, *"It's time."*

But the truth doesn't force itself forward.
It waits for our permission.
It asks: *Will you let me come through with love?*

This is the voice of awakening. Not the voice that wants to impress, convince, or prove—but the voice that simply wants to be real.

If you've struggled to find your voice or feared being misunderstood, you are not alone. Many of us were taught that truth-telling had to be harsh or dramatic to be effective. But there is another way.

You can speak your truth without raising your voice.
You can share your frequency without explaining your beliefs.
You can lead with light, even in hard conversations.

The invitation now is not to become louder.
It's to become clearer.
More attuned.
More willing to feel your words before you speak them

Soul Reflection

- What truth am I ready to speak—but afraid to name?
- Where have I been using words to protect myself, rather than express myself?

- What would it feel like to speak with love, even when it's hard?

The Frequency That Speaks for You

The world doesn't need more noise.
It needs clarity.
It needs truth wrapped in compassion.
It needs your voice—aligned, awake, and free.

Not the version of you that's edited for acceptance or armored by past wounds.
The real you. The steady you. The soft-but-unshakable you.

Because when we speak from presence, we don't just express our truth—we **transmit it**. We allow our words to carry the frequency of love, not just the facts of our lives. We speak not to impress, but to illuminate. To invite. To remember.

So the next time you feel the nudge to say something that matters—pause.
Not to silence it, but to feel its frequency.
And then speak with the fullness of who you are.

Let your voice be a tuning fork for truth.
Let your words be the doorway through which your soul enters the room.
Let your frequency do the speaking—because when it does,
the right people will always hear you.

But even the clearest voice has its edges.

Even the most resonant truth eventually dissolves into mystery.

Because not everything within you is meant to be spoken—not yet.
Some truths live between the words.

Some wisdoms arrive not in declarations, but in stillness.

And sometimes, the most sacred invitations come wrapped in silence—disguised as confusion, doubt, or the ache of not knowing.

There comes a moment on the spiritual path when words begin to feel too small.

When explanations no longer satisfy.

When the voice you've worked so hard to trust gently hands the journey over to something deeper.

This is not the end of your voice.

It's the widening of it.

And in the space beyond words—where certainty slips away and clarity hasn't yet arrived—another kind of wisdom waits.

It doesn't rush.

It doesn't shout.

But if you listen closely, it will lead you.

In the pages ahead, we'll follow that guidance—into the quiet terrain where trust becomes the only map, and the unknown reveals itself not as a threat, but as a sacred homecoming.

Into the Deep— Trusting the Unknown

"The greatest discoveries are found not in what is known but in the courage to explore what lies beyond."

Have you ever felt a pull toward something you couldn't quite explain? Maybe it was a whisper, a nudge, or an unshakable curiosity. The unknown has a way of calling us, inviting us to step beyond the edges of our comfort zones. It's both exhilarating and terrifying because stepping into the unknown means letting go of control. But here's the thing: the unknown isn't something to fear—it's a doorway to transformation.

I've always believed that life's most profound lessons come from the moments when we say "yes" to the mystery. One such moment happened to me on a wall dive in the Cayman Islands, and it forever changed the way I view the unknown.

A Manta Ray in the Deep Blue

The water was crystal clear that day, and the visibility was so sharp that I felt like I could see forever. My dive group and I were exploring one of the island's famous wall dives, where the coral reef plunges into a deep blue abyss. The wall was mesmerizing—alive with vibrant corals and darting fish. It was easy to get lost in its beauty, completely absorbed in the intricate details unfolding before me.

But then, something strange happened. I felt a quiet but insistent pull to turn around. At first, it didn't make sense. Why would I look behind me? The wall was where all the action was, and beyond it was just an endless, empty ocean. Still, the feeling wouldn't go away, so I gave in.

And there it was.

In the vastness of the deep blue, a giant manta ray appeared in the distance, gliding effortlessly through the water. Even from afar, its wings seemed to span forever—each movement a silent symphony of grace and knowing. Its presence was humbling, not just for its sheer size, but for the way it seemed to embody the very essence of mystery. Here was this magnificent creature, emerging silently from the emptiness, carrying with it a sense of wonder that defied words.

Time seemed to stand still as I watched, suspended between awe and disbelief. The manta ray moved with an otherworldly rhythm, disappearing slowly into the blue depths until it faded like a ghost into the ocean's embrace. In its departure, it left something more—a quiet imprint on my soul. It was as if the universe had whispered, "See? This is what happens when you trust."

In that moment, I realized the pull I had felt wasn't random—it was the universe guiding me toward something profound, a reminder that life's most extraordinary moments often arise when we trust and follow our intuition.

I've often wondered how many moments like this we miss in life—the ones that require us to step outside our assumptions and trust what we cannot see. It wasn't just a choice to turn around; it was a choice to trust that there was meaning beyond the familiar.

The Nature of Mystery—Learning to Turn Toward What We Cannot See

Mystery is an integral part of life, yet it's something we're often taught to avoid. Society conditions us to seek certainty, to plan, to know. But the truth is, life doesn't come with guarantees. The unknown is always present, whether we acknowledge it or not.

What if, instead of resisting it, we saw mystery as a trusted companion? Much like the manta ray in the deep, it exists to remind us that there is always more to life than what we can see, plan, or control.

The irony is that some of life's greatest gifts are hidden within the unknown. It's not a void to be feared; it's a space of infinite possibility. When we embrace mystery, we open ourselves to experiences and insights we could never have imagined.

That dive taught me an invaluable lesson: sometimes, life calls us to look behind or beyond what's immediately in front of us. The manta ray reminded me that beauty and wisdom often reside in the places we least expect. But to experience them, we must trust enough to look beyond our comfort zones and release the need for control.

In many ways, life is like that wall dive. We become so focused on the path right in front of us that we forget to explore the vastness all around us. We resist the pull to step into the unknown because it feels safer to stay where we are.

But what if, like the manta ray, something extraordinary is waiting just beyond our line of sight?

The Rewards of Trusting the Mystery

When we surrender to the unknown, transformation finds us. Our connection to ourselves, others, and the world deepens in ways we could never have planned. We discover new perspectives, hidden strengths, and unexpected joys.

For me, the manta ray became a symbol of grace and flow. Its movements were effortless, a reminder that life doesn't have to be a constant struggle. When we trust the mystery, we align with a rhythm that carries us, much like the ocean carries its creatures.

Practical Tools for Embracing the Unknown

Embracing the unknown doesn't mean abandoning all logic or preparation. It's about balancing faith with action and curiosity with courage. Here are a few tools to help you trust the mystery:

Reflect on Moments of Trust:

Think about a moment in your life when you stepped into the unknown and discovered something beautiful. What called you to take that step? What did you learn about yourself or life in the process?

Practice Presence:

The unknown feels less intimidating when we stay grounded in the present moment. Focus on what's here and now.

Follow Intuition:

Pay attention to those quiet nudges and gut feelings. Whether it's a feeling that nudges you to take a different route home or an idea that seems to appear out of nowhere, intuition often leads us to extraordinary discoveries.

Cultivate Curiosity:

Approach the unknown with wonder instead of fear. Ask questions, explore possibilities, and remain open.

Surrender and Flow:

Trust that life has a way of unfolding perfectly, even when it doesn't go according to your plan.

The Gift of the Mystery—
Listening for the Divine Whispers

I think about that manta ray often. It appeared in a moment when I wasn't looking for it, when I had no reason to expect anything extraordinary. It was a moment that changed something in me—quietly but forever.

The mystery of life is like that—unexpected, awe-inspiring, and full of grace. It asks us to trust, to turn toward it, and to embrace its vastness. When we do, we find that the unknown isn't empty at all. It's brimming with possibilities, waiting for us to take the leap.

The universe is always speaking; the question is, are we listening?

When we trust the mystery, we open ourselves to a profound dialogue with the universe. It communicates in subtle yet powerful ways—a fleeting thought, the lyrics of a song that feel written just for us, or an unshakable nudge toward a path we can't yet see. These aren't coincidences. They're whispers of the divine, bypassing logic to speak directly to the soul.

The manta ray wasn't just a breathtaking creature; it was a message. A reminder that guidance often comes when we least expect it, cloaked in mystery and daring us to notice. The universe rarely shouts or offers step-by-step instructions. Instead, it offers symbols, synchronicities, and quiet nudges, asking us to pause, listen, and trust.

When we learn to tune into these whispers, life transforms. The ordinary becomes extraordinary, and we begin to see that the universe weaves meaning into the fabric of our lives. A recurring symbol, a persistent idea, or even the quiet pull to turn toward the unknown—all of these are invitations to engage with the divine.

But recognizing that guidance requires stillness. It requires presence. And most of all, it requires trust.

Mystery invites us to surrender and listen, to notice the synchronicities and moments of unexplainable clarity that point the way. These whispers aren't always loud or obvious. They often live in the quiet spaces—waiting for us to pay attention.

When we do, we discover that we are never walking alone.
The unknown isn't empty.
It's sacred.
It's alive.
And it's already speaking.

As we listen more deeply, something else begins to emerge—not answers, but awareness. A widening. A softening. A space where what we once called "the unknown" becomes something far more sacred. In the next chapter, we'll step into that space—not to define it, but to dwell in it. To become the stillness that listens, and the presence that remembers what lives beyond the need to know.

The Sacred Unknown—
Becoming the Space Between

"The void is not your enemy—it is your invitation to become."

There is a space on the path of awakening that no one really prepares you for.
It isn't dramatic or awe-inspiring. It doesn't arrive with fanfare or clarity.
It shows up quietly—after the shedding, but before the becoming.
A space between stories. Between selves. Between identities.

It feels like emptiness, but it isn't empty.
It feels like stillness, but something is stirring.
And it feels like silence, yet it hums with a presence just beyond perception.

This is the sacred unknown.
And if you're in it, chances are, your mind is trying to get out.

The Discomfort of Being Nowhere

We are trained to fear the in-between.

In a world that worships certainty, productivity, and progress, it's easy to mistake stillness for failure. When we're not moving forward, defining goals, or checking boxes, something inside us starts to panic.
What am I doing with my life?
Why isn't anything happening?
Shouldn't I know by now?

But the sacred unknown isn't a mistake in your journey—it's a threshold.

It's the cocoon between the caterpillar and the butterfly, the moment between inhale and exhale, the seed underground before it ever breaks the surface. It's the moment the universe asks you to stop seeking... and start listening.

Not to a voice.
Not to a sign.
But to **space** itself.

Why the Unknown Feels So Unbearable

The sacred unknown is not painful because of what it is.
It's painful because of what it isn't.

It doesn't give us answers.
It doesn't offer timelines.
It doesn't validate who we thought we were—or tell us who we're becoming.

It asks us to wait. To trust. To soften into something we can't yet see.

And for the mind, that feels unbearable.

This is the place where many people turn back.
They try to force the next step, chase a new identity, or grab onto the nearest certainty just to avoid the discomfort of not knowing.
But the sacred unknown cannot be bypassed. It can only be entered.

And it's not passive. It's profoundly alive.

This space is not empty—it's creative. It's where old stories lose their grip, but new ones have not yet taken form.
It's the moment before the insight, before the call, before the clarity.

In spiritual terms, this is the void.

But not the void of despair—the void of potential.
The fertile ground where your next chapter is quietly gestating, preparing to rise—not from force, but from alignment.

It's not a punishment.
It's a pause on purpose.

The Times I Tried to Skip This Part

I've tried to outrun the void more than once.

There have been seasons where everything I thought I knew began to dissolve—my direction, my clarity, even my sense of self. And instead of trusting the unfolding, I went into fix-it mode. I signed up for new trainings, built new offers, filled my calendar with action... all so I wouldn't have to feel the discomfort of not knowing.

But nothing aligned.
The energy wasn't there.
The clarity didn't come.

It was as if life itself was holding up a mirror, whispering: *You're not supposed to know right now.*
Not because I was doing something wrong. But because something deeper was trying to emerge.

And emergence can't be rushed.

It took me time—and a few hard lessons—to realize that forcing clarity before it's ready doesn't make things move faster. It just creates resistance.
But when I finally surrendered, softened, and stopped trying to label what was happening, something subtle began to shift.

Not in the outer world.

In me.

There was no dramatic breakthrough. No lightning bolt of insight. Just a quiet sense that I was being held—even here. Even in the pause.

And in that stillness, I began to feel something ancient. Something sacred.
Like I was being rearranged from the inside out, not for performance, but for alignment.

It wasn't comfortable. But it was holy.

Trusting the Sacred Space Between

If you're in a season of uncertainty right now—where the path feels unclear, the inspiration quiet, or your inner compass seems to have gone still—please know this:

You are not broken.
You are becoming.

You're not off track.
You're in the space between tracks—where the next step is being written by a part of you that doesn't speak in words.

This isn't the time to rush forward.
This is the time to soften inward.

To trust that something deeper is moving, even if you can't name it yet. To allow the unknown to be a companion, not a threat.

If life feels paused, it's because something is preparing to move through you—not from strategy, but from soul.

This moment is not meaningless. It is sacred reorganization.

Soul Reflection

- Where in my life am I being asked to pause, but I keep pushing?
- What would it feel like to stop searching for the next answer—and trust that it's already unfolding?
- Can I let the unknown be a teacher, instead of something to solve?

When Stillness Begins to Speak

We often think of guidance as a voice—a sign, a message, a clear direction. But in the sacred unknown, guidance arrives differently.

It doesn't always come as a lightning bolt or a loud knowing.
Sometimes it's a breath.
A shift in energy.
A quiet curiosity pulling you somewhere new without explanation.

It may not feel like guidance at all.
But that's only because you've been trained to look for clarity, not resonance.

And yet, as you soften into the unknown, something extraordinary begins to happen.

What once felt like silence begins to shimmer with presence.
What once felt like emptiness begins to hum with meaning.

You begin to notice subtle invitations—glimpses, sensations, synchronicities.
A remembered dream.
A feather on your path.
A sentence that lands differently, as if written just for you.

And you realize:
The unknown was never empty.

It was always speaking.

You were simply becoming quiet enough to hear it.

In the pages ahead, we'll begin to tune in—to recognize the whispers already woven into your daily life, and learn how to walk beside them with trust.

Whispers of the Divine—Finding Guidance in Everyday Life

"The divine speaks not in thunderclaps but in whispers. To hear it, we must quiet our minds and open our hearts."

There was a time in my life when I began noticing something unusual—numbers. Not just any numbers, but the same ones appearing over and over. At first, I dismissed it. A coincidence, I thought. But as the days went on, it became impossible to ignore. I would glance at the clock and see 3:33. The next day, it was 2:22 on a receipt. Another time, 11:11 blinked at me from my phone screen. It felt as though the universe was speaking—gently, consistently—urging me to listen.

I didn't know it then, but I was beginning to learn how to hear its whispers—the subtle ways it nudges us, invites us, and aligns us with something greater. The numbers were just the beginning.

As they continued to appear, I couldn't help but wonder if there was meaning behind them. Curiosity got the better of me, and I began to pause and look into the messages these numbers might hold. As I mentioned earlier, I quickly discovered that these repeating numbers are often referred to as "angel numbers," each carrying its own message. The 3s, for instance, are said to symbolize alignment with divine energy and encouragement to express yourself fully. The 2s signify balance and trust in the unfolding of your journey. Every time I saw these numbers, I took a moment to reflect on what was happening in my life.

It was in those pauses that I began to sense something deeper—an invitation to trust the unseen threads weaving through my days. The whispers of the universe were not random; they were part of a larger tapestry, nudging me toward alignment with my highest self.

Those moments of reflection became little touchstones—opportunities to slow down and listen. It wasn't just about the numbers anymore. It was about tuning into a deeper sense of guidance. The more I paid attention, the more these signs seemed to show up, weaving their way into my everyday life. It was as if the universe was speaking to me, not through thunderclaps or grand gestures, but through these quiet, gentle nudges, urging me to trust that I was being supported.

This experience opened a door to something much greater: the understanding that divine guidance is always present. The whispers of the universe come to us in countless ways—through symbols, synchronicities, and even the still, small voice within us. What's required is not a special ability but a willingness to pay attention, to pause and notice what is already there.

You don't have to be someone who "sees signs everywhere" to recognize this guidance. Chances are, the universe has already been speaking to you. Maybe it's through a song lyric that answers a question you've been pondering, or a random nudge that urges you to call someone at just the right moment. These whispers are gentle but persistent, and when we learn to listen, they can transform how we move through the world.

In this chapter, we'll explore how to recognize and trust these divine whispers, learning to attune to the guidance available to us in every moment. Because the universe is always speaking—the question is, are we ready to listen?

Recognizing the Whispers

Have you ever felt like the universe was trying to tell you something? Maybe it's the way a particular song seems to follow you everywhere or how a random conversation answers a question you've been wrestling with. These moments can feel small, almost insignificant at first. But when you start to notice them, they begin to form a pattern, as if the universe is whispering directly to you.

The truth is, the divine is always communicating with us, offering guidance, comfort, and direction. It's not through grand gestures or booming voices but through subtle, meaningful moments—a kind of divine language woven into the fabric of our everyday lives. Once you start paying attention, you'll find these whispers all around you, inviting you to trust the journey you're on.

These two forms of guidance—external synchronicities and internal intuition—are like twin flames, working in harmony to lead us closer to our truth. The synchronicities grab our attention, while intuition helps us understand their meaning. Together, they form a divine language, guiding us through life's uncertainties with clarity and trust.

The Dance of Synchronicity

Synchronicities are one of the clearest ways the universe communicates. These are those uncanny "coincidences" that align so perfectly with your life that they feel anything but random. I learned this lesson when I was just 17, though at the time, I didn't realize it was the universe whispering to me.

Like most teenagers, I thought I had everything figured out. I already knew which three colleges I would apply to, and that was that. My high school counselor, however, kept insisting that I apply to a fourth school—just to keep my options open. I resisted, stubbornly clinging to my plan. I didn't see the point in applying anywhere else.

One afternoon, I was sitting in my counselor's office when something unusual happened. Out of nowhere, a college catalog quite literally jumped off the shelf and landed at my feet. The school was Siena, a college I'd never heard of and certainly wasn't interested in. He raised an eyebrow, clearly amused. Frustrated, I picked up the catalog and said, "Fine, I'll apply to this one," more out of irritation than curiosity. I had no intention of even considering it. In my mind, it was just a formality to appease him.

Fast forward a few months, and I found myself on a road trip with some friends, visiting colleges one of them was interested in. As we drove down the highway, we decided, on a whim, to pull off and grab something to eat. While navigating the unfamiliar streets, we happened to pass a sign for Siena College. "Hey, isn't that the school you said you were applying to?" someone asked from the back seat.

Curious, we decided to swing by and check it out. I still remember the moment we drove onto the campus. The soft rolling hills seemed to invite us in, and the people we encountered were so kind and welcoming that they left a mark on me. There was something about the energy of the place—it felt peaceful like it was waiting for me.

In that moment, I realized that divine guidance often works through what seems like chance. Each "coincidence" is a thread connecting us to the larger story of our lives, inviting us to trust in the unseen.

Suddenly, the school I had dismissed without a second thought became my first choice. I knew the second I stepped onto that campus that this was where I was supposed to be.

Looking back, it's so clear to me how the universe orchestrated the whole thing. From the catalog falling off the shelf to the spur-of-the-moment decision to get off the highway, each "coincidence" was a divine nudge, guiding me to exactly where I needed to be.

Moments like these remind us that life is not random. Synchronicities are evidence of a divine choreography, working behind the scenes to align people, places, and events in ways we could never plan ourselves. All we have to do is trust those moments when the universe seems to tap us on the shoulder and say, "Pay attention—this is for you."

But not every synchronicity feels grand or life-changing. Sometimes, the whispers of the universe come through in small but equally meaningful ways—subtle nudges that remind us we're always supported, even in the little things.

For instance, one morning, I was frantically searching for a document I needed for an important meeting. After turning the house upside down with no luck, I paused, took a deep breath, and asked the universe for help. Within moments, I felt a nudge to check a drawer I hadn't considered. There it was, exactly where I needed it to be. It may seem like a small thing, but in that moment, it felt like the universe was gently reminding me, "I'm here."

The Quiet Voice of Intuition

If synchronicities are the universe's external nudges, intuition is the quiet inner voice guiding you from within. That gut feeling, that quiet knowing that defies logic but feels undeniably true, is one of the most powerful ways the universe communicates with us.

Intuition isn't loud; it's subtle, like the faintest melody humming beneath the noise of everyday life. When we cultivate stillness, that melody becomes clearer, guiding us with wisdom that words cannot convey.

Think of the last time you had an instinct about something—a strong nudge to follow a certain path or avoid a situation. Maybe you felt compelled to call a friend and later found out they really needed someone to talk to. Or perhaps you made a decision that didn't make sense on paper but turned out to be exactly right. These moments are not accidents. They are your soul tuning in to the frequency of divine guidance.

One of the most profound lessons I've learned is that intuition doesn't shout. It whispers. And if we're too busy or distracted, we can easily miss it. That's why creating space for stillness is so important. When we slow down, that quiet voice within becomes clearer, and we can begin to trust it more fully.

Learning to Pay Attention

The first step in recognizing the whispers of the divine is simply learning to pay attention. Our lives are filled with distractions—emails, deadlines, notifications—and it's easy to overlook the subtle ways the universe is trying to guide us. But when you make a conscious effort to notice, you'll start to see the signs everywhere.

Ask yourself:

- Have you experienced any "coincidences" lately that felt too meaningful to ignore?
- Are there moments when your intuition has nudged you in a certain direction?
- What symbols, patterns, or events keep catching your attention?

Sometimes, it helps to keep a journal of these moments. Write down the synchronicities, intuitive hits, or small, meaningful occurrences you experience, no matter how insignificant they seem. Over time, you'll start to notice patterns—a divine roadmap guiding you toward your truth.

A Gentle Invitation

The whispers of the divine aren't reserved for a select few. They are available to all of us, every single day. Whether it's through a serendipitous moment, the quiet voice of intuition, or the perfect message arriving at just the right time, the universe is constantly inviting us to listen, trust, and take the next step.

It's not about searching for these moments but about being open to noticing them. So the next time something catches your attention—a random comment, an unexpected opportunity, or an inner nudge—pause and ask yourself: "What is the universe trying to tell me?"

When you create space to listen, you'll discover that guidance has been there all along, patiently waiting for you to notice.

Trusting the Guidance

Recognizing the whispers of the universe is only the first step. The real transformation begins when we learn to trust them. And let me be honest: trusting divine guidance isn't always easy. It often challenges our logic, pushes us out of our comfort zones, and asks us to step into the unknown.

The whispers rarely come with guarantees. They don't say, "If you follow this nudge, everything will work out exactly as you want." Instead, they invite us to take a leap of faith, to listen to the quiet voice within even when the world around us is loud with doubt.

The Struggle Between Logic and Intuition

We live in a society that values reason and practicality, so when divine guidance nudges us in a direction that doesn't make logical sense, it's easy to ignore or second-guess it. But the whispers of the universe don't operate on human logic—they operate on a higher wisdom that sees the full picture, even when we cannot.

One of the toughest decisions I ever made was to end a relationship with someone I deeply cared about because it had become toxic. Her actions were impacting my mental health, and as much as I didn't want to let go, I knew I had to. Everything in me resisted—I felt guilty, conflicted, and even selfish—but deep down, my intuition was clear: this relationship wasn't healthy for me anymore.

A year passed, and I had made peace with the decision. Then one day, seemingly out of nowhere, the phone rang. It was her. I almost didn't pick up, but something inside me said, "Answer it." When I did, I learned that she was going through an incredibly difficult time and had no one else to turn to.

In that moment, I realized that while our relationship had ended, the universe had brought us together again for a reason. I was able to help her navigate that challenging season of her life, providing support when she needed it most. And when that season ended, we naturally drifted apart again.

Trusting that nudge to answer the call wasn't easy. It brought up old wounds and fears. But I also saw the bigger picture: sometimes, divine guidance isn't about rekindling what was but about showing up in love, even for a brief moment.

How to Build Trust

Learning to trust divine guidance is like strengthening a muscle—it takes practice and consistency. Here are a few ways to deepen your trust:

Reflect on Past Nudges: Look back on times when you followed an intuitive nudge or a sign and it led to something meaningful. What did you learn from that experience? Let those moments serve as proof that you can trust the whispers.

Start Small: You don't have to make life-changing decisions right away. Practice following smaller nudges, like reaching out to someone, taking a different route home, or saying yes to an unexpected opportunity.

Embrace Uncertainty: Trusting guidance often means stepping into the unknown. It's not about being fearless but about choosing faith over fear, one step at a time.

Ask for Clarity: If you're unsure about a nudge, don't be afraid to ask the universe for confirmation. Sometimes, additional signs will appear to reassure you that you're on the right path.

Celebrate Alignment: When you trust a whisper and it leads to something positive, celebrate it! Acknowledge the divine guidance at work and thank the universe for its support.

A Leap of Faith

When we trust the whispers, we're not just placing faith in the universe; we're placing faith in ourselves and our ability to navigate life in partnership with the divine. Trusting guidance doesn't guarantee a smooth ride, but it does ensure we're walking the path meant for us.

So, the next time you feel that quiet nudge or see a sign that resonates, pause and ask yourself: "What's the worst that could happen if I follow this? And what might happen if I don't?" More often than not, the risk of listening is far outweighed by the gift of alignment.

The whispers of the universe are always inviting us to step into something greater. Trust them. You might not see the full picture now, but when you look back, you'll see how every step was leading you home.

Strengthening Your Connection

Recognizing the whispers of the divine and learning to trust them are transformative steps, but the journey doesn't stop there. Like any meaningful relationship, our connection with the universe deepens when we nurture it. The more intentional we are about fostering this bond, the clearer and more frequent the guidance becomes.

Think of your connection with the divine as a two-way conversation. The whispers may be subtle, but they're always present. Our role is to cultivate the practices, mindset, and stillness that allow us to hear them more clearly.

Gratitude Opens the Door

One of the simplest yet most powerful ways to strengthen your connection is through gratitude. When we acknowledge the signs, synchronicities, and intuitive nudges we receive, it's like saying, "I see you. Thank you."

I'll never forget a time when I felt overwhelmed by doubt. I wasn't sure I was on the right path, and I asked the universe for a sign—anything to let me know I wasn't alone. Not long after, I received exactly what I needed: an unexpected opportunity that perfectly aligned with my goals. In that moment, I felt immense gratitude, not just for the opportunity but for the reminder that I was supported.

The more I've practiced gratitude for these moments, the more they seem to appear. It's as though the universe responds to our acknowledgment by opening the door wider, saying, "Here's more guidance, since you're paying attention."

Start small. At the end of each day, reflect on any signs or moments of connection you experienced, no matter how subtle they seemed.

Gratitude shifts your focus and helps you notice even more of the divine at work in your life.

Daily Rituals for Connection

Another way to attune to the divine is to create daily rituals that center you and invite stillness. When we rush through life, it's easy to miss the whispers entirely. By carving out intentional time each day, we create space for those whispers to reach us.

Here are a few simple rituals to consider:

Morning Meditation: Begin your day with a few moments of quiet reflection. Focus on your breath, set an intention, and ask the universe to guide you. Even five minutes can shift your energy.

Mindful Walks: Take time to spend in nature and notice the beauty around you. The divine often speaks through the natural world—through the rustle of leaves, the flight of a bird, or the warmth of the sun.

Journaling: Keep a journal where you write down your thoughts, questions, and any signs or synchronicities you notice. Over time, patterns may emerge that reveal a deeper truth.

Evening Reflection: Before going to bed, take a moment to reflect on your day. Ask yourself, "Where did I feel the presence of the divine today?" This simple question trains your mind to notice the guidance you may otherwise overlook.

These rituals don't have to be complicated. The key is consistency and intention. The more space you create for connection, the stronger it becomes.

Clearing the Path

Just as clutter in our physical space can create chaos, energetic clutter can block our connection with the divine. Strengthening your bond often requires clearing away what no longer serves you—whether that's limiting beliefs, unresolved emotions, or relationships that drain your energy.

Take a moment to reflect:

- Are there beliefs holding you back, like "I'm not worthy of divine guidance" or "It's just a coincidence"?
- Is your schedule so packed that you have no room for stillness or reflection?
- Are there toxic patterns or relationships that cloud your ability to trust your intuition?

Clearing the path isn't always easy, but it's essential. When you release what weighs you down, you create space for the whispers of the universe to reach you.

Tuning into the Present Moment

The divine doesn't live in the past or the future—it speaks to us in the present moment. Yet, so often, we're too distracted to notice. We're replaying old conversations in our minds or worrying about what's coming next, all while missing the signs right in front of us.

Strengthening your connection means practicing presence. It's about slowing down, being here, and now. When you're fully present, the whispers become clearer.

Here's a simple practice to try:

- The next time you're in a moment of stillness—whether sipping your morning coffee, watching a sunset, or sitting in silence—take three deep breaths.

- As you breathe, focus on what's around you: the sounds, the colors, the sensations.
- Ask yourself, "What is the universe showing me in this moment?"

You might not receive an immediate answer, and that's okay. The act of pausing and tuning in is enough to strengthen your awareness.

Becoming a Co-Creator

As you strengthen your connection, you'll notice a shift. You're no longer just receiving guidance; you're co-creating with the divine. Your actions, intentions, and gratitude align with the whispers, creating a flow where life feels less like a struggle and more like a partnership.

The whispers of the universe don't disappear when life gets hard—they often grow louder. By creating space, expressing gratitude, and staying present, you'll find that your connection deepens, guiding you through even the most challenging moments.

The divine is always reaching out to you. Strengthening your connection is simply a matter of reaching back.

Living in Harmony with the Divine

When we recognize the whispers of the universe and trust their guidance, something extraordinary begins to happen: life starts to flow. It's not that challenges disappear or that every day feels effortless, but there's a sense of alignment—a deep knowing that you're not walking alone. Instead, you're in partnership with something greater, co-creating a life of purpose, connection, and grace.

Living in harmony with the divine is like stepping into a dance. The music has always been playing; we're simply learning to move with it. The more we lean into this rhythm, the more attuned we become to its direction.

Flowing with Grace

There's a beauty in living in sync with divine guidance. It's the feeling you get when things effortlessly fall into place, when a seemingly random opportunity turns out to be exactly what you needed, or when you follow a quiet nudge and it leads to an unexpected blessing.

I've had moments in my life where I felt completely aligned, as though an invisible current was carrying me. One particular summer stands out: every decision I made, every step I took, seemed to unfold perfectly. At the time, I was dedicating myself to daily rituals of reflection, gratitude, and listening. I was intentional about creating space for the whispers to reach me.

During that summer, I noticed how even the smallest choices seemed to lead to profound outcomes. A casual conversation would open the door to a new opportunity. A delay that felt frustrating in the moment would turn out to be a blessing. It was as though the universe was saying, "Trust me—I've got you." And the more I trusted, the more I saw evidence of that truth.

Living in this kind of harmony doesn't mean life is free of challenges, but it does mean facing those challenges with faith and support. You begin to see that even the obstacles have purpose, guiding you to grow in ways you couldn't have anticipated.

Listening Beyond the Noise

Harmony with the divine doesn't happen by accident. It requires us to actively choose presence over distraction, faith over fear, and gratitude over doubt. In a world full of noise, this can feel like swimming upstream, but it's worth the effort.

The whispers of the universe are quiet by nature. They are not meant to compete with the chaos around us; they are meant to guide us back to ourselves. This is why creating stillness in our lives is so vital. Whether through meditation, prayer, or simply spending time in nature, these moments of quiet allow us to reconnect with the divine and hear the whispers more clearly.

Ask yourself:

- When was the last time I truly slowed down and listened?
- How can I create more space in my life for stillness?
- What might I hear if I let the noise fade into the background?

The answers to these questions can help you cultivate a deeper sense of harmony, where you feel not just guided but held.

Co-Creating with the Universe

As we strengthen our connection to the divine, something magical happens. We begin to see how our choices and actions weave together with the whispers of the universe to create the life we're meant to live. This isn't a passive process where we sit back and wait for signs to lead the way. It's an active, dynamic partnership—one where our willingness to take a step forward allows the universe to align the path ahead.

Think of it like planting a garden. The universe provides the soil, the sun, and the rain, but it's up to us to plant the seeds, tend to the weeds, and nurture what we've sown. Together, we co-create something beautiful, something that could never exist without this collaboration.

This process isn't always about knowing exactly where you're going. In fact, some of the most profound moments of co-creation happen when we embrace the unknown. When we trust the whispers without needing all the answers, we create space for the divine to work its magic.

Living as a co-creator means showing up each day with intention, faith, and action. It's a dance of give and take, listening and responding, trusting and doing. When we embrace this dance, we discover a life that feels deeply aligned, purposeful, and filled with unexpected grace.

A Life of Trust and Joy

When we live in harmony with the divine, life becomes less about striving and more about flowing. We begin to see each moment—whether joyful, challenging, or mundane—as part of a greater story. We trust that the whispers will guide us, even when the path ahead is unclear.

Imagine waking up each day with the confidence that you are supported, guided, and loved by something far greater than yourself. Imagine navigating your challenges with faith, knowing that every twist and turn has meaning. This is what it feels like to live in harmony with the divine.

And here's the most beautiful part: when you align with the whispers, you also align with your highest self. The guidance you receive isn't separate from you—it's a reflection of the divine spark within you.

An Invitation to Dance

The whispers of the universe are always there, inviting us to dance, trust, and co-create. They are woven into the fabric of our lives, gently reminding us that we are never alone.

So, the question isn't whether the universe is guiding you. It always is. The question is: Are you willing to listen? Are you willing to trust? And are you willing to take that next step, knowing you are held every step of the way?

Living in harmony with the divine is a journey, not a destination. It's about showing up daily with an open heart and a willing spirit. And when you do, you'll find the dance more beautiful than you ever imagined.

Trusting the Whispers

As we learn to recognize and trust the whispers of the divine, a sense of partnership begins to take root. These whispers become our compass, guiding us through moments of doubt and uncertainty, offering clarity when the way forward seems unclear. Living in harmony with this guidance isn't just about hearing the divine; it's about learning to move with it, to trust that each nudge is leading us exactly where we need to be.

But guidance isn't meant to live only in our meditations or journals.

It's meant to shape how we show up in real time—in our relationships, our decisions, and the quiet in-between moments that make up our lives.

As we step into *Part 5: Timeless Tools for Transformation*, we begin with a return to embodiment. Not lofty ideals, but lived truth. Not someday... but now.

Awakening is no longer a concept.
It's becoming a practice.
And the next chapter invites you to begin living it—moment by moment, breath by breath.

PART 5
Timeless Tools for Transformation

"The tools of transformation are timeless because they anchor us in the eternal. In stillness and storms, they remind us that peace, clarity, and divine strength are always within reach."

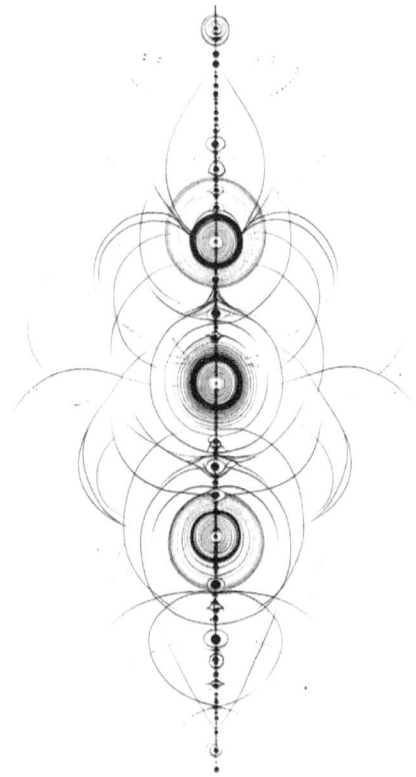

Living the Light—
Awakening in Real Time

*Awakening doesn't ask you to leave the world behind—it asks you
to meet it with new eyes and a steady heart."*

There's a myth we often carry—sometimes silently—that one day we'll
finally "arrive."
That awakening will click into place like a finished puzzle, and life will
suddenly make perfect sense.
But the truth?
Awakening doesn't happen all at once. It unfolds in real time.

In the middle of our errands.
In the pause before we react.
In the moment we remember to breathe instead of brace.
In the way we show up when no one's watching.

Awakening isn't about floating above the chaos.
It's about choosing to bring your light into it.
To let the divine shape your decisions, not just your meditations.

What It Means to Live Your Awakening

There's a difference between awakening as a moment—and awakening
as a lifestyle.

You can have a powerful realization on your yoga mat, in nature, or
during a deep meditation. But the real work begins when you try to carry
that awareness into a Monday morning meeting... or a family dynamic
that hasn't evolved... or the checkout line when you're running late and
the cashier is moving at the speed of molasses.

Living your light means allowing your inner transformation to reach your outer actions.

It's easy to feel spiritually aligned when you're alone in sacred space. But what about when you're exhausted, triggered, or misunderstood? What about when nothing is going your way?

That's when awakening becomes a choice.

To pause before reacting.
To speak from alignment instead of defense.
To notice your patterns and gently disrupt them with compassion.

You don't have to be perfect.
You just have to be willing.

Because spiritual awakening isn't an identity—it's a daily invitation.

When Life Gave Me the Perfect Test

I didn't know it at the time, but the moment I hit the edge of the bathtub, everything shifted.

One minute I was moving through the final draft of this book—completely immersed, completely in flow. I had worked eighteen hours the night before without even realizing how late (or early) it had become. It felt effortless in the moment, but my body was running on empty.

So I decided I'd take a long, grounding soak in the tub—Epsom salts, candlelight, a moment to reset.

I sprayed the tub with cleaner first, as I often do, letting it sit while I jumped back into editing just *one more* section.
But four hours passed.
I was so deep in the work that I completely lost track of time.

By then, the day had moved on. I no longer had time for the soak I'd planned.

I turned on the shower instead—rushed, distracted, ungrounded.

The cleaners were still there. So was the slippery surface beneath me.

And then—

In one swift, sobering moment, I crumpled into a heap in the tub.

Cracked ribs.

Sharp pain.

Breath knocked out of me—literally and energetically.

I couldn't move without hurting. And yet what hurt even more was the realization that I had bypassed all the things I say I stand for: presence, embodiment, energetic integrity.

I'd been teaching flow. Talking about balance. Writing about alignment.

And there I was—pushing, rushing, overriding every signal from my own body.

The universe didn't need to shout.

It just needed to knock the breath out of me long enough for me to listen.

And in that stillness—when I couldn't do anything but lie there and feel—it hit me:

I wasn't living my awakening.

I was running past it.

Choosing Alignment in the Ordinary

You don't need a fall to remind you to slow down.

You don't need a crisis to choose your presence.

But sometimes the soul will let the body speak loudly—when it's the only way we'll hear.

Living your light isn't about transcending your human life.
It's about infusing it—with truth, with intention, with grace.

It's pausing before you say yes out of habit.
It's noticing when your body contracts and asking what it needs.
It's leaving space between your breath and your reaction—so your soul can speak first.

You don't need to be "high vibe" all the time.
You just need to be honest.
Present.
Willing to notice when you've slipped into the current of old patterns—and loving enough to guide yourself back.

That's what living your awakening looks like.
Not a constant state of enlightenment, but a thousand small moments of remembrance.
Moments where you choose presence over pressure.
Compassion over performance.
And alignment over autopilot.

Soul Reflection

- Where in my life am I performing presence but avoiding embodiment?
- What does alignment feel like *in my body*—not just in my thoughts?
- What would change if I let awakening become a practice, not a performance?

Awakening in Motion

Living your light isn't about getting it right every time.
It's about noticing sooner when you've drifted... and choosing to return.

Again and again.

That return is the practice.
That return *is* awakening.

It doesn't always look like action.
Sometimes the most aligned thing you can do—is pause.

Because when you stop running from the discomfort, the silence becomes sacred.
And in that stillness, something ancient awakens.
A deeper intelligence.
A deeper peace.

In the space ahead, we'll explore what it means to find calm in the very center of the chaos—
To let stillness become not just a break in the noise, but a portal to the divine.

The Eye of the Storm—Finding Peace in Stillness

"Stillness is not the absence of movement but the presence of peace, where the soul whispers and the divine speaks."

Let me ask you something: When was the last time you truly stopped? Not just physically, but mentally and spiritually?

Think about the moments when life feels the most chaotic—when your mind races, and the demands of the day seem endless. It's in those moments, ironically, that something sacred begins to emerge. Not in the doing, but in the stopping. That's when we begin to feel it: the power of the pause.

Pausing isn't about escaping; it's about returning—to your breath, your center, and the truth of who you are.

If you're anything like me, the idea of stopping—really stopping— might feel foreign, maybe even a little uncomfortable. I get it. We live in a world that rewards doing. From the moment we wake up, there's always something demanding our attention: emails to answer, meals to make, family to care for. We wear our busyness like a badge of honor, but deep down, we know it comes at a cost.

For years, I was swept up in that current, too. It wasn't until life pressed pause on me—when exhaustion and overwhelm left me no choice—that I discovered the power of stillness. I remember sitting down one day, feeling completely drained, and for the first time in what felt like forever, I did nothing. No emails. No tasks. I just sat there with myself.

At first, my mind rebelled. "You're wasting time," it scolded. "You're lazy. You should be doing something." That voice—so familiar, so relentless—had lived in my head for years, echoing the unkind words I'd once believed about myself. For so long, it had driven me to push harder, do more, and prove my worth. Sitting still felt almost unbearable, as if by stopping, I was confirming every negative thing I'd ever been told.

But something shifted as I stayed there. Slowly, the storm in my mind began to settle. The voice grew quieter, and in the stillness, something new emerged—a sense of peace I hadn't felt in years. It wasn't loud or overwhelming, but soft and steady, like the warmth of sunlight breaking through clouds. It reminded me that I was alive, whole, and connected to something greater than my thoughts, my fears, or the stories I'd carried for so long.

That moment wasn't just a pause—it was a turning point. In the quiet, I began to hear a deeper truth, one that had been waiting patiently beneath the noise: I am enough.

As I sat in stillness, I realized I wasn't alone in this struggle. So many of us are caught in the same cycle of busyness, yearning for peace but unsure how to find it. That was the moment I discovered something I want to share with you: stillness isn't a luxury; it's a lifeline. It's where we reconnect with the essence of who we are. I call it the sacred pause, and it's a gift I now treasure—one I hope you'll embrace, too.

The Modern Addiction to Movement

We live in a culture that glorifies busyness. Productivity is praised, and rest is often treated as laziness. Even as children, we're taught to equate worth with achievement—getting good grades, excelling in sports, meeting expectations. Over time, this conditioning becomes a pattern, leading us to measure success by how much we accomplish rather than how connected we feel to ourselves and others. From the moment we wake up to the second we fall asleep, we're bombarded with notifications, to-do lists, and the endless pursuit of "more."

It's no wonder so many of us feel disconnected and drained. We've been conditioned to believe that our worth is tied to what we achieve, so we keep moving, doing, and striving—afraid that if we stop, we'll fall behind.

But here's the irony: the more we run, the further we drift from what truly matters. In our quest to do it all, we lose touch with ourselves, our purpose, and the divine wisdom that can only be heard in the quiet.

Stillness is not the enemy of progress. It's the foundation of it. When we pause, we allow our minds and souls to catch up with our lives. We create space for clarity, insight, and renewal. The sacred pause isn't about stopping everything; it's about remembering what's essential.

What would it feel like to give yourself permission to pause, even for just a moment?

Stillness as Sacred Space

Imagine a raging storm—wind howling, waves crashing, chaos everywhere. Now picture the calm center of that storm, where the air is still and everything feels clear. Stillness offers us a sacred space at the center of life's chaos, where we can reconnect with our true selves and the divine.

This sacred space isn't something external—it exists within each of us. It's the part of ourselves that remains unshaken, even when life feels overwhelming. When we enter this space, we don't deny the storm; we acknowledge it while grounding ourselves in the calm that allows us to navigate it.

Throughout history, spiritual leaders and mystics have recognized the power of stillness. Yeshua retreated to the wilderness to pray and reflect, and monks have long practiced silence to commune with the divine. Even in nature, we see this truth: the most profound growth often occurs in quiet moments.

Stillness isn't about doing nothing; it's about being fully present. It's in those moments of pause that we hear the gentle whispers of our soul and the guidance of something greater. When we allow ourselves to be still, we enter into a sacred conversation with the divine—a space where answers emerge, wounds begin to heal, and clarity unfolds.

Embracing the Pause in Daily Life

You might wonder, "This all sounds great, but how do I make time for stillness in a life that feels anything but still?" The beauty of stillness is that it doesn't demand dramatic changes to your routine. It's about weaving moments of presence into the life you already have. Even a few seconds of presence—a deep breath, a moment of mindful awareness— can ripple peace through your entire day.

The truth is, you don't have to retreat to a monastery or spend hours meditating to embrace the sacred pause. Stillness is a practice, and it can be woven into the fabric of your daily life.

Here are a few ways to begin.

I know many of these may feel familiar—and that's intentional. Some of the most powerful practices are the simplest ones, and they're worth repeating. These moments of stillness aren't just good habits—they're anchors. Quiet touchstones that realign you with peace before the world rushes in.

Morning Stillness: Start your day with a few moments of quiet. Before you reach for your phone or dive into the day's tasks, sit in silence. Breathe deeply, and set an intention for the day.

Mindful Transitions: Use the spaces between activities—like the commute to work or the time before a meeting—to pause and center yourself. Picture this: instead of filling the commute with noise, you allow yourself a moment to reflect, letting the world slow down around you.

Breath Awareness: When stress arises, return to your breath. Inhale deeply, exhale slowly, and allow yourself to feel grounded in the present moment.

Journaling: Take a few minutes each evening to write down your thoughts, feelings, and insights. This practice helps you process your day and connect with your inner self.

Gentle Movement: For those who find stillness challenging, practices like yoga or mindful walking can be a bridge to quieting the mind.

You don't have to get it perfect. The beauty of the sacred pause is that it's always available to you, no matter how busy or chaotic life feels.

The Transformative Power of Stillness

What happens when we embrace stillness? Each person's answers are unique, but one truth remains universal: stillness changes everything. In stillness, we begin to notice what we've overlooked—the quiet beauty of the present moment, the strength we've carried through difficult times, and the wisdom that comes from simply being. Stillness doesn't erase life's challenges; it equips us to face them with greater clarity and resilience.

In the quiet, we rediscover who we are beneath the layers of expectation and busyness. We hear the inner wisdom that's been waiting patiently for our attention. We connect with the divine in a way that transcends words.

I remember a particularly difficult season of my life when everything felt uncertain. I had questions with no answers and fears that seemed insurmountable. But in the moments when I allowed myself to pause, I felt a deep knowing that I wasn't alone. In those sacred pauses, I found the strength to take the next step, even when I couldn't see the whole path.

Stillness isn't just a gift we give ourselves; it ripples outward. When we're grounded in peace, we bring that peace into our relationships, our work, and our world.

Living in the Pause

Here's the beautiful truth about the sacred pause: it doesn't demand perfection. It simply invites presence. Whether it's five minutes in the morning, a deep breath in a moment of stress, or a quiet walk in the evening, the pause reminds us of what truly matters.

You don't need to escape to a mountain retreat or clear your calendar to find stillness (though if you can, it's wonderful!). The sacred pause meets you where you are, exactly as you are. It's about creating space for your soul to breathe amidst the demands of life.

Even if your mind wanders or you feel restless, simply pausing is enough. Each attempt to pause strengthens your connection to the present moment, building a foundation of peace that grows stronger with time.

Stillness, like the calm eye of a storm, reminds us that no matter how turbulent life becomes, there is always a place of peace within.

The Calm Before the Storm

Stillness, however, is just the beginning. Life will always bring storms—those inevitable moments that challenge our strength and shake our foundations. Yet, it is in the sacred pause where we discover the quiet resilience within us—the calm center that steadies us when life's winds howl.

But here's the gift of stillness: it doesn't make the storms disappear, but it anchors you through them. The calm you cultivate in the sacred pause becomes a wellspring of inner strength, reminding you that even in the chaos, peace is always within reach.

As we step forward, we'll explore the spiritual tools that anchor us in these turbulent times, helping us navigate life's storms with unwavering peace and grace. Because the stillness we cultivate now becomes the strength we carry into the challenges ahead.

Anchored in the Storm—Tools for Resilience and Renewal

"Life's storms will come, but peace is not found in avoiding the chaos—it's found in anchoring yourself to the calm within."

Imagine standing in the middle of a storm. The winds rage, rain lashes against your skin, and the world around you feels like it's falling apart. Yet, deep within, there's a calm—a place untouched by the chaos. This inner calm is not something reserved for the enlightened or the lucky—it's a universal gift we all carry within us. It is the whisper of your soul reminding you that no storm lasts forever and that you are stronger than you realize. Can you picture it? A moment where, despite everything happening around you, you feel steady, grounded, and at peace.

For most of us, that sense of calm feels elusive during life's storms. When challenges hit—whether it's a difficult relationship, a health scare, financial strain, or even global uncertainty—it's easy to feel swept away. But what if I told you that it's possible to anchor yourself no matter how fierce the winds get?

The storms of life aren't meant to destroy us; they're meant to shape us. They clear away what no longer serves us, uproot what needs healing, and prepare us for new growth. Still, weathering them requires tools—a spiritual toolkit to keep us grounded, resilient, and aligned.

In this chapter, we'll explore practical and spiritual tools for staying anchored during turbulent times. From grounding techniques to the healing power of vibrational frequencies, meditation, and surrender, these practices are designed to help you face any storm with grace and strength.

The Nature of Life's Storms

Challenges are part of the human experience. Life's storms come in waves—sometimes gentle enough to nudge us, other times crashing with the force of profound change. These storms test our resilience and show us where our foundation may need strengthening. None of us are immune to them. They come in many forms—some as gentle rain, others as full-blown hurricanes. But no matter their size, they have one thing in common: they bring change.

Think about the last significant challenge you faced. Maybe it felt like everything was crumbling, and you weren't sure how you'd get through it. But here you are, on the other side, stronger and wiser than before. That's the gift of life's storms—they teach us lessons we couldn't learn in calmer waters.

Storms often feel chaotic and destructive, but they also create space for renewal. Just as a tree bends in the wind to avoid breaking, we're meant to adapt and grow through our challenges. And like a tree, we need strong roots—practices that keep us grounded even when life feels unpredictable.

Grounding—The Foundation of Inner Calm

In moments of chaos, our minds often race, caught up in worst-case scenarios or overwhelmed by uncertainty. Grounding is not about escaping these thoughts but gently bringing ourselves back to the present, where clarity and peace can be found. It is one of the simplest and most powerful tools we have during turbulent times. It's the practice of reconnecting to the present moment and stabilizing ourselves emotionally, physically, and spiritually. When the world seems to be spinning out of control, grounding reminds us that we are safe, steady, and capable of weathering the storm.

There have been times in my own life when I've felt unmoored, like the storm was too great to endure. On days like these, I turn to nature. It's my practice to walk barefoot outside, feeling the coolness of the earth or the softness of the sand beneath my feet. These simple acts connect me to the present moment. I often joke, "I need my fix," if I miss a day or two of quality time in nature because, for me, being in nature is a form of meditation. It's in these quiet moments, with the breeze on my skin and the grounding connection to the earth, that I rediscover my inner peace.

There are many ways to ground yourself and anchor your energy during turbulent times. Here are a few practices to try:

Physical Grounding *(my favorite!)*: When you feel overwhelmed, try connecting to the earth. Take off your shoes and walk barefoot on grass or soil. Let your senses guide you: feel the texture beneath your feet, smell the air, and listen to the sounds around you.

Energetic Grounding
Imagine roots growing from the soles of your feet deep into the earth, anchoring you to its core. Visualize the earth's energy rising through those roots, filling your body with stability and strength.

Emotional Grounding
Sometimes, we need to ground our emotions. Try this: place your hand over your heart, close your eyes, and take three slow, deep breaths. Repeat a calming affirmation like, "I am safe. I am steady. I am enough."

Movement
For those who find stillness challenging, practices like yoga or mindful walking can be a bridge to quieting the mind.

Quick Practices for Grounding and Surrender

Grounding practices are like anchors in the storm—small but mighty tools that keep you steady when the world feels unstable. These rituals don't have to be grand or time-consuming; their power lies in their simplicity and consistency. Here are some additional ways to make grounding a daily ritual, even during the busiest days:

Morning Ritual

Start your day with intention. If possible, step outside and connect with nature—even a few moments of fresh air can create a powerful shift. As you breathe, repeat the affirmation:

"I am safe. I am steady. I am supported."

Mini-Meditations

Set a timer for two minutes, close your eyes, and focus solely on your breath. Inhale peace, exhale tension. Even a few minutes can calm your energy and reset your focus.

Affirmations for Resilience

Place sticky notes around your space as loving reminders. Some examples:

- "I trust the process of life."
- "I am anchored in peace."
- "This storm is shaping me into something stronger."

Grounding isn't about doing it perfectly—it's about returning to presence. Even in the busiest seasons, these small rituals offer calm, clarity, and resilience. When woven into your day with intention, they become touchstones of strength to carry you through any storm..

The Healing Power of Frequencies

We are vibrational beings at our core, with every cell, organ, and system in our bodies resonating at specific frequencies. This symphony of vibrations creates the energetic blueprint that supports our physical, emotional, and spiritual well-being. When life's challenges knock us off balance, sound and frequency can act as powerful tools to bring us back into alignment.

Frequencies have been used throughout history for healing and transformation. Ancient civilizations intuitively understood the power of sound. From the chants of Tibetan monks to the rhythmic drumming of Indigenous tribes, sound has been a sacred bridge between the physical and the spiritual. Even today, science is beginning to validate what these traditions have known for centuries: sound affects the mind, body, and soul. Studies on sound therapy have shown its ability to lower stress, improve focus, and even promote healing at the cellular level.

The beauty of sound lies in its accessibility. Different tones and vibrations can shift our energy and restore harmony. Music, for instance, can instantly change your mood—a soothing melody can calm your nerves, while an uplifting rhythm can inspire you to move. This is the power of sound at work, influencing both our emotions and energy in profound ways.

Sound frequencies work on a deeper level, resonating with the mind, body, and spirit. These vibrations interact with your energy field, helping to clear blockages, balance your system, and create a sense of calm. The effects depend on the type of frequency you use.

For example, gentle, low tones are grounding and stabilizing, ideal for calming anxiety or helping you feel centered during stressful times. Higher, more uplifting tones can energize and elevate your spirit, helping you connect with higher levels of awareness and creativity. By understanding how different frequencies affect your energy, you can use sound as a powerful tool for healing and transformation.

You don't have to be an expert in sound therapy to experience its benefits. You can explore simple tools like singing bowls, tuning forks, or guided meditations tuned to specific frequencies. These accessible practices allow you to bring the healing power of sound into your everyday life, offering balance and renewal no matter where you are.

Sound Healing Tracks

Find music or guided meditations tuned to specific healing frequencies. Simply listening to these can help balance your energy, calm your mind, and promote harmony in your body. Here are some examples of frequencies and their potential effects:

- *174 Hz:* Known as a soothing frequency, it helps relieve pain and tension in the body, offering a sense of safety and security.
- *396 Hz:* A grounding frequency that helps release fear, guilt, and other heavy emotions, making it excellent for emotional cleansing.
- *432 Hz:* Often called the "universal frequency," this frequency is believed to align with the universe's natural resonance, fostering relaxation, balance, and inner peace.
- *528 Hz:* Sometimes referred to as the "Love Frequency," it is associated with DNA repair, transformation, and the activation of positive energy.
- *639 Hz:* A frequency that supports heart-centered communication, helping to heal and strengthen relationships with yourself and others.
- *852 Hz:* This frequency is ideal for meditative and reflective practices. It is known for awakening intuition and promoting spiritual insight.

These frequencies can be found in many forms: instrumental tracks, nature-inspired soundscapes, or music infused with these tones. Apps, streaming platforms, and sound healing playlists make it easy to access tracks specifically tuned to these frequencies. As you listen, notice how your body and mind respond—it might surprise you how deeply the right frequency resonates with you.

By exploring these frequencies, you're giving yourself a simple yet profound tool for navigating life's storms, helping to restore balance and peace within.

Singing Bowls or Chimes

These ancient tools produce pure, resonant tones that seem to reach right into your soul. Singing bowls—crafted from crystal or metal—emit vibrations that do more than sound; they harmonize your energy field and soothe your nervous system. When played, they create a sound that isn't just heard but felt, reverberating through your body and encouraging deep relaxation.

Chimes, with their light, ethereal tones, work in a similar way, often used to clear energetic blockages and refresh the space around you. Both tools are perfect for moments when you need to reset your energy, whether during meditation, at the end of a stressful day, or when creating a calming atmosphere in your home. Simply strike a chime or gently play a singing bowl, and let its soothing sound guide you back to balance and alignment.

Your Own Voice

You carry one of the most powerful healing tools within you: your voice. Humming, chanting, or toning creates vibrations that resonate directly through your body, calming your nervous system and grounding your energy. These vibrations stimulate the vagus nerve, a key player in relaxation and emotional regulation. They help reduce stress and foster a sense of inner peace.

For example, humming softly to yourself can quickly shift your energy, especially in moments of anxiety or overwhelm. Chanting mantras like "Om," "Ah," or "Hum" can connect you to deeper spiritual states while aligning your energy. You don't have to be a singer or even chant in a particular tradition—what matters is the intention and the resonance you feel.

Your voice is a direct link to your energy and emotions, and when you use it consciously, it can become a steady anchor, guiding you back to your center during turbulent times.

The Power of Meditation and Surrender

Meditation is often described as a refuge, a place where we can retreat from the chaos of life and reconnect with the divine. But for me, it's more than that—it's an anchor. It is also a practice of empowerment, teaching us that even amidst the storm, we can find strength within ourselves. Meditation is not about silencing the chaos but learning to observe it without being consumed by it. When the storm outside feels overwhelming, meditation brings me back to the still, quiet center within myself.

Here's a simple meditation to try:

- Sit comfortably, close your eyes, and focus on your breath.
- As you inhale, imagine peace entering your body.
- As you exhale, release tension and worry.
- If your mind wanders (and it will), gently guide it back to your breath.

Meditation doesn't have to be perfect; it just has to be honest. Even a few minutes of stillness can calm your mind and reconnect you with your inner strength.

Another powerful practice during turbulent times is surrender. This doesn't mean giving up or ignoring the storm; it means releasing the need to control every outcome and trusting that the divine is guiding you.

I've had moments where surrender felt like my only option. Times when I didn't have an answer or a clear path forward. In those moments, I would close my eyes, place my hands over my heart, and say, "I release this to you. Show me the way." And somehow, the way always appeared—not because I forced it, but because I let go.

Building Resilience Through Faith

Resilience is the ability to keep standing, even when the winds howl and the rain pours. It is the quiet voice within that says, *You've been here before, and you made it through.* Resilience isn't about never falling—it's about rising every time you do.

Faith plays a big role in building resilience. I'm not just talking about religious faith, though that can be part of it. I'm talking about faith in something bigger than yourself—faith in the divine, in the process of life, and in your own strength.

One way to build resilience is through daily affirmations. Try starting your day with statements like:

- "I am strong enough to face this storm."
- "I trust the process of life."
- "I am anchored in peace."

Gratitude is another powerful tool. Even in the midst of challenges, there's always something to be thankful for—a sunrise, a kind word, a moment of stillness. Gratitude shifts your focus from fear to abundance, reminding you that even in the storm, there is light.

From Storms to Sunlight— Reclaiming the Inner Light

Each storm we endure shapes us, polishing away the fear and doubt to reveal the unshakable light within. This light guides us forward, reminding us that every storm carries the seed of transformation.

Through the storms of life, we've learned to find the calm within—a sanctuary of peace, resilience, and strength. By grounding ourselves, embracing the healing power of frequencies, and surrendering to the flow of life, we've discovered that the chaos around us does not define us. These tools have not only helped us weather the storms, but also prepared us for what comes next: the joyful return to wholeness.

Because beyond resilience lies something even more luminous—the part of us untouched by hardship, still brimming with creativity, curiosity, and wonder. It is the voice of the inner child.

In the next chapter, we'll explore how reconnecting with this vibrant, unburdened part of ourselves can awaken a deeper sense of joy and authenticity. When we honor the wisdom of our inner child, we don't just recover from the storm—we rise into the light.

The Inner Child's Song—A Journey to Reclaim Joy

"Reclaiming your joy begins with remembering who you were before the world told you who to be. Listen to your inner child—they hold the map back to your truest self."

If you could go back and speak to your younger self, what would you say? What words would you offer to comfort them, guide them, or remind them of the light they carried—even when the world seemed determined to dim it?

For me, this question isn't hypothetical. I've spent much of my adult life revisiting the voice of my younger self—trying to understand her pain and rediscover the joy that had been buried beneath it. At the heart of it all was **a forgotten voice**—my own—but one that struggled to be heard.

When I first started speaking, no one could understand me. My words tumbled out in a way that only my brother, Leo, could decipher. My mother tells the story of me crying in my carriage, fussing with frustration, and Leo translating for me: "The sun is in her eyes." He was my voice before I had one the world could understand.

As I grew, the struggle became more visible—and more painful. It wasn't just that my words were hard to understand; it was the way others reacted that hurt the most. What began as innocent confusion from classmates turned into teasing, and eventually, outright ridicule. Even some of the adults around me didn't know how to meet me with compassion.

The next thing I knew, I was sitting outside the principal's office while my mom, Helen, and my first-grade teacher—who later became my "Aunty Pat"—discussed my speech therapy. They were worried. Not just about my words, but about the way Mrs. Y's insults—"stupid" and "dumb"—were beginning to take root in my mind.

Those words left a mark. They weren't just something I heard; they became something I believed. For years, the mantra played in my head: *You're lazy. You're stupid. You're dumb.* It affected everything—how I spoke, how I showed up in the world, how I saw myself.

And yet, beneath the pain and the layers of self-doubt, there was still a spark of joy. That spark—the voice of my inner child—wasn't gone. She was waiting for me to find her, to heal her, and to let her speak again.

Meeting the Inner Child

The inner child is the part of us that carries our earliest experiences. They hold our first moments of wonder and joy, but also our wounds and fears. For me, my inner child carried both the playful girl who laughed with her brother and the scared little girl who thought her voice didn't matter.

When we're young, we absorb the words and actions of others like sponges, forming beliefs about ourselves and the world. For me, the speech disorder wasn't just a physical challenge—it became a lens through which I saw myself. The ridicule from others, and the hurtful words overheard from adults, reinforced that lens.

These beliefs don't simply disappear as we grow up. Instead, they shape our choices, our relationships, and the way we speak to ourselves. For years, I pushed myself to prove I wasn't lazy or stupid. I worked hard, achieved goals, and became more "productive" than ever—but the voice of that little girl, still scared and hurting, lingered just beneath the surface.

Reconnecting with her—listening to her, understanding her pain— became a turning point. For me, this journey involved journaling and visualization, but it's important to remember that the process looks different for everyone. Some may find connection through creative outlets, others through meditative walks in nature, or even conversations with trusted loved ones. The essential part is allowing space for your inner child's voice to emerge in a way that feels right for you.

One of the first steps I took to reconnect with my inner child was through journaling. I started by writing down memories from my childhood—moments of joy, moments of pain, and even seemingly insignificant details like what I loved to play with or how I felt about certain places. As I wrote, patterns began to emerge. I noticed how often I felt the need to be perfect, how much I feared disappointing others, and how deeply those fears were rooted in the belief that I wasn't enough.

Visualization also became a powerful tool in this journey. I would close my eyes and imagine myself as a little girl, sitting cross-legged in the middle of a sunlit field. I pictured myself walking toward her, sitting down beside her, and holding her hand. Sometimes, she would look at me with tears in her eyes, and I would tell her, "It's okay. You're safe now. I'm here." Other times, she would laugh, and I would feel her joy ripple through me, reminding me of the light that still lived within us.

These small but profound practices helped me identify the moments where I had buried my feelings—times when I had told myself, *This doesn't matter* or *I'll deal with this later.* By bringing those moments into the light, I began to understand how they shaped my adult fears, insecurities, and self-perceptions.

Reconnecting with my inner child wasn't about fixing her—it was about honoring her. Each time I engaged in these activities, I felt closer to the playful, creative, and courageous girl I had once been. And with every step, I found myself reclaiming the parts of me I thought I had lost.

Writing a Letter to Your Younger Self

One day, over lunch, I opened up to Aunty Pat about how much that conversation outside the principal's office had hurt me. To my surprise, she remembered it well. She explained that she and my mom were heartbroken, worried that I was beginning to believe Mrs. Y's taunts. "We never thought you were lazy or dumb," she said. "We were just so afraid you'd start believing it."

Hearing that was healing. It was as though her words rewrote part of my story, softening the edges of old wounds I had carried for decades. For the first time, I saw that the people who truly loved me had never seen me the way I had seen myself—as someone less than. But healing didn't happen all at once. While her affirmation cracked open the door, the real transformation began when I sat down to write a letter to my younger self.

In the summer of 2024, Aurora Luna Star suggested I try this exercise: "Write a letter to your younger self. Tell her what you wish you could've said back then." At first, I resisted. The idea of confronting that pain felt overwhelming. Would writing to her open old wounds I wasn't ready to face? Or worse, would it confirm the beliefs that had haunted me for so long?

Eventually, I mustered the courage to try. I set aside a quiet afternoon, lit a candle, and placed a photo of myself as a little girl beside me. Staring at her face—those wide eyes filled with both curiosity and vulnerability—I began to write.

The words came slowly at first, but as I let my emotions guide me, the floodgates opened. I told her everything I wished someone had told her back then:

"You are not lazy, stupid, or dumb. You are brave. You are creative. And your voice matters—more than you know."

I acknowledged her pain, validating the experiences she had endured. "I know how hard it was when people didn't understand you, and I know how much it hurt when they called you names. You didn't deserve that. None of it was your fault."

As I wrote, I felt an overwhelming sense of tenderness toward her. I told her how proud I was of her for persevering, even when the world felt unkind. I reminded her of the joy she brought to those who loved her and assured her that her struggles would one day become her strength.

Writing that letter wasn't just an act of kindness—it was an act of reclamation. With each sentence, I felt a weight lifting, as though I was pulling pieces of myself out of the darkness and back into the light.

When I finished, I read the letter aloud. Hearing those words spoken brought a new level of healing. It was as though I was giving voice to the little girl who had once felt silenced, letting her know she was no longer alone.

That simple act of writing became a gateway to healing, and it reminded me how powerful words can be in transforming pain into strength. If you're ready to connect with your inner child, writing a letter can be a beautiful first step.

How to Write a Letter to Your Inner Child

Writing a letter to your inner child can be a powerful and transformative exercise. Here's a simple guide to help you get started:

Create a Quiet, Safe Space

Find a peaceful spot where you won't be interrupted. Light a candle, play soft music, or surround yourself with objects that bring you comfort.

Visualize Your Younger Self

Close your eyes and imagine yourself at a specific age or moment in your childhood. Picture how you looked, what you were wearing, and how you felt. Let this image guide you.

Start with Compassion

Begin the letter with kind, reassuring words, as if you're comforting a dear friend. Let your younger self know that they are loved and safe.

Acknowledge Their Struggles

Reflect on the challenges they faced, validating their feelings. Avoid minimizing or dismissing their pain. This is your chance to let them feel seen and heard.

Offer Encouragement and Support

Share what you admire about them and how they inspired the person you've become. Let them know their struggles didn't define them and that they have always been enough.

End with Love and Gratitude

Close the letter by expressing gratitude for their strength and resilience. Reaffirm your connection with them and remind them that their joy and light still live within you.

Read it Aloud (Optional)

If it feels right, read the letter aloud to yourself. This can deepen the emotional impact and help you internalize the healing words.

Remember, there's no right or wrong way to do this exercise. Write from your heart, and let the words flow naturally. Even if it feels awkward at first, trust the process—it's part of the journey.

Reclaiming Playfulness and Joy

One of the most profound ways I reconnected with my inner child was through rediscovering my love of dance. As a little girl, I loved how dancing made me feel—free, expressive, and alive. Somewhere along the way, life's responsibilities pushed that joy aside.

When I was young, ballet and tap classes were my sanctuary. The stage was magical, and the freedom of movement let me express emotions words couldn't. Every week brought the excitement of learning new routines, and the end-of-year recitals were the pinnacle of joy. The costumes were dazzling, the stage enchanting, and for those few minutes of performing, my shyness melted away entirely.

The fifth year of dance brought an even greater sense of anticipation, as this recital came with a special milestone: a trophy to celebrate five years of participation. I couldn't wait to wear my costume, take the stage, and finally receive my award alongside my classmates. I still remember the butterflies in my stomach as we waited backstage, listening as names were called one by one.

But then, as the line moved forward, something shifted. They called the "C's," and my heart raced. Any second now, I thought. Then the "T's" came and went, and I was still standing there, clutching my excitement like a balloon slowly deflating in my hands. I must have been invisible because no one saw me. No one noticed that I was still there, alone in the wings, waiting to be seen and acknowledged. The show ended with the director receiving a bouquet of roses, and I just stood there, unseen.

I don't remember much after that, but I know my mom must have dashed out of her seat to say something because the next thing I recall is being brought on stage, where the director graciously handed me her roses. I know now that it was an act of kindness, but my nine-year-old self didn't see it that way. To her, it was proof of what she'd already suspected: she didn't belong, she wasn't meant to be seen, and she didn't matter as much as everyone else.

That moment stayed with me for years, shaping how I saw myself. The girl who loved to dance, who had once felt joy in every movement, became the girl who doubted her worth. But even then, the spark of joy wasn't completely extinguished—it was just waiting for me to find it again.

This past summer, as I reconnected with my inner child, I wrote another letter, this time to my nine-year-old self. I told her how proud I was of her for dancing her heart out, how she mattered so much more than she realized, and how she had every right to be seen, celebrated, and loved. That letter became another step in my journey to reclaim joy—not just for my younger self, but for the woman I had become.

Reconnecting with dance as an adult felt like reclaiming a part of myself. It wasn't just about the steps—it was about the joy, the freedom, and the connection to a younger version of me who was still waiting to be acknowledged. Rediscovering joy isn't always easy, but it's essential. Whether it's dancing, painting, or simply playing in the grass, reconnecting with the things that made you happy as a child can open the door to healing. Your inner child is still there, waiting to guide you back to the wonder and creativity you once knew.

The Power of Forgiveness

Forgiveness played a pivotal role in my journey to reclaim joy—especially forgiving myself for the years I believed I was broken. Writing to my inner child helped me acknowledge her pain, but I also needed to extend that same compassion to myself as an adult.

One practice that helped me was mirror work. I stood in front of the mirror, looked into my own eyes, and said affirmations like, "I love you. I forgive you for the times you doubted yourself. I honor the courage it took to heal." At first, it felt awkward, but over time, I began to see myself through kinder eyes.

Forgiveness doesn't erase the past; it releases its grip on the present, allowing space for growth and joy to re-enter. Each time I forgave myself, I noticed small but profound shifts—moments where old wounds softened, and I felt more at ease with who I was becoming. This practice became a bridge, connecting me not only to my inner child but also to the person I was learning to be: someone whole and free.

Embracing the Joy Within

Rediscovering joy isn't just about healing wounds; it's about choosing to live vibrantly. As adults, we often lose touch with the wonder we felt as children. But that wonder still lives within us, waiting to be awakened.

The journey to reclaim joy doesn't have to be overwhelming—it begins with small, intentional steps that resonate with your unique experiences. For some, this might mean revisiting hobbies you loved as a child, like drawing, playing an instrument, or exploring nature. For others, it could involve trying something entirely new—an art class, a dance workshop, or even planting a garden. The key is to follow what feels lighthearted and authentic to you. These seemingly small actions can reignite the spark of curiosity and creativity that lies within you.

Creating rituals for playfulness can also help infuse joy into your daily life. Consider setting aside time each week for an activity that feels lighthearted and fun. For me, this meant scheduling "dance breaks" throughout my week. I'd put on my favorite music and let myself move freely, just as I did when I was a little girl. These moments reminded me that joy doesn't have to be complicated—it's often found in the simplest acts of letting go.

Laughter, too, is a powerful way to invite joy back into your life. Try watching a favorite comedy, playing a silly game with your loved ones, or even recalling a funny memory from your past. Laughter has a way of breaking down walls, releasing tension, and reminding us that life isn't meant to be taken too seriously.

Another small but impactful practice is keeping a "joy journal." Each evening, write down one thing that brought you happiness that day. It could be as simple as the taste of your morning coffee, a kind word from a stranger, or the sound of birds outside your window. Over time, this practice trains your mind to notice and appreciate the little moments that make life beautiful.

Healing and joy often go hand in hand. By taking these small, intentional steps, you begin to create space for the lighthearted, unburdened version of yourself to emerge. And as you nurture that part of yourself, you'll find that joy becomes not just an occasional experience, but a way of being.

Healing the Wounds, Reclaiming the Voice

For years, I believed my voice didn't matter. The speech disorder, the ridicule—it all felt like proof that being heard wasn't for me. But as I've peeled back the layers of this wound, I've discovered something powerful: My voice does matter. And so does yours.

Reclaiming your voice doesn't mean erasing the pain of the past. It means honoring it, learning from it, and using it to speak your truth with courage and confidence.

Forgiveness has been a key part of this journey—not just forgiving others, but forgiving myself for the years I believed those hurtful words. Each layer of healing brings me closer to wholeness, closer to the joy I thought I'd lost.

A Journey Back to Joy

This chapter marks a turning point in our journey—one where healing opens the door to joy, and where remembering who we truly are becomes the light that guides us forward. Your inner child, with all their wonder, creativity, and light, is still within you. Their voice matters. Their joy matters. And when you honor that part of yourself, you don't just heal—you rediscover the fullness of life.

Reclaiming joy is not about forgetting the struggles or bypassing the pain; it's about weaving those experiences into the fabric of who you are and choosing to live vibrantly despite them. It's about recognizing that the wounds you once carried—including the times when your voice may have felt silenced—have shaped your strength, your wisdom, and your ability to shine.

As I reflect on my own journey, I think back to the little girl who struggled to find her words, who often felt unseen and unheard. She is still a part of me, and today, I carry her voice forward—not with fear, but with pride. She has taught me that joy is not about perfection, but about presence. About rediscovering the freedom to speak, to love, and to live authentically.

So I invite you to pause and reflect: What would your younger self say if they could see you now? Would they be proud of the life you've built, the lessons you've learned, and the love you've allowed into your heart?

Perhaps they'd whisper, "Thank you for finding me again."

In this moment, promise yourself to carry their light forward. Laugh freely, love deeply, and never stop exploring the wonder that still surrounds you. Let your inner child remind you that life is meant to be lived with joy—not just in fleeting moments, but in the everyday magic of being alive.

And so, I'll leave you with this:

The path to joy is not a straight line. It twists and turns, inviting you to grow, to heal, and to become. But no matter where the road leads, joy is always within reach. It is the voice of your soul calling you home.

A Return Beyond Healing

As we reclaim the joy of our inner child—alive, playful, and unburdened— we do more than heal the past.
We open a gateway.

Because within the laughter, the lightness, and the sacred permission to be fully ourselves...
there is something deeper still: a memory waiting to rise.
A soul song older than time.

As we enter *Part 6: Echoes of the Eternal,* the journey shifts once more.

What if the light you carry wasn't just meant to awaken you...
but to awaken the world around you?
Not through explanation.
But through presence.

Not through seeking.
But through becoming.

In the pages ahead, we move beyond the boundaries of story—into a remembrance that lives not in the mind, but in the frequency of who you are.

Not to escape this life.

But to embody it fully—as the light being you've always been.

PART 6
Echoes of the Eternal

"We do not end. We return.
To the stars, to the stillness, to the truth that never left us."

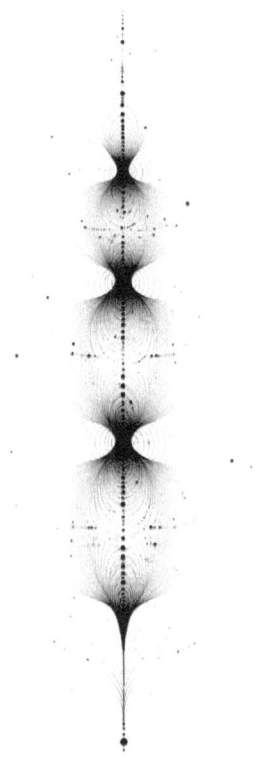

The Voice of the Cosmos—
Embodying Galactic Lineage

"You are not just remembering where you've been. You're remembering why you came."

There are moments when you don't just hear truth—you *feel* it echo through your cells.

It bypasses logic.
It skips the need for explanation.
It moves like music you somehow know by heart, even if you've never heard it before.

That's what happened the first time I heard the words *Sirius C.*
No preamble. No proof. Just a frequency that rang through my entire body with the clarity of something long forgotten, finally remembered.

The voice didn't come from outside me.
It came *through* me.
And suddenly, I wasn't just receiving cosmic insight. I was becoming it.

We talk a lot about remembering in spiritual circles—but what if remembrance is not just about reclaiming the past?
What if it's about *activating* what you came here to anchor?

You didn't just come to *know* the light.
You came to *embody* it.
To carry codes that were never meant to stay hidden.

And now... it's time to let them speak.

Remembering Is Not the Same as Embodying

It's one thing to feel connected to the stars—to have moments of recognition when you hear about the Pleiades, Sirius, Andromeda, or Arcturus.

It's another thing entirely to *live* as someone who carries that frequency.

We aren't here to collect galactic names like spiritual credentials.
We're here to ground a frequency of love, wisdom, and ancient knowing into this present, messy, human world.

Galactic remembrance isn't about escaping Earth—it's about returning to it with clarity and purpose.

That's what *embodiment* means.

It's not about having vivid visions or recalling every past life. It's about how you move through this one.
How you speak.
How you hold presence.
How you love.
How you listen to guidance that doesn't make sense but never steers you wrong.

You may never "know" all the details of where you're from.
But you'll feel it in how you lead.
In how you resonate with truth.
In the way you *carry light*—not just in your beliefs, but in your being.

Because you didn't come here to impress anyone with cosmic knowledge.
You came here to shift the frequency of Earth.

And that doesn't happen in theory.
It happens in how you live.

You Are the Transmission

There's a moment in the awakening journey when the need to "figure it all out" gives way to something quieter—but more powerful.
Not a search for the story, but a return to the frequency.

Over time, I've come to understand that galactic remembrance isn't about gathering more information—it's about becoming the vibration you already carry.
It doesn't ask to be explained.
It asks to be embodied.

Because when you remember... the invitation becomes to live it.

The cosmic voice doesn't want to be admired or analyzed. It wants to be embodied.

It doesn't need us to prove our lineage or explain our origin story.
It asks us to embody the frequency we were born to carry.

That's the new leadership.

Not louder.
Not more polished.
Not cloaked in light to avoid the dark.

But rooted. Resonant. Willing to hold steady in a world still waking up.

This isn't the kind of leadership that comes with a stage.
It comes in how you hold space in a difficult conversation.
In how you stay open when others shut down.
In how you honor your knowing—even when no one else understands it.

You don't have to "sound spiritual" to embody your mission.
You don't have to channel publicly or name your star system.

You just have to live aligned.

Present. Awake.

Soft in your power and steady in your light.

Because when you walk as the frequency—when you *are* the vibration you came to Earth to bring—you activate others by your very presence.

The Light That Walks Among Us

Not every galactic soul came to be known.

Many came simply to hold the grid.

To hum softly in rooms where hearts are breaking.

To smile in ways that remind people who they really are.

You may be one of them.

If so, please know: your quiet is not a flaw.

Your subtlety is not a weakness.

Your doubt does not disqualify you.

The very fact that you feel this chapter in your bones is evidence of your remembrance. You didn't arrive late to this awakening—you arrived right on time.

You are here because Earth needs your frequency now.

Not to escape the world—but to help recreate it.

You are the encoded light of galaxies past...

and the seed of futures not yet imagined.

You are not here to wait for permission.

You are here to live your truth—so fully, so gently, so completely—that it awakens others to their own.

And when the light within begins to hum louder than the doubt...

When the whispers no longer ask to be interpreted but *followed*...
When the codes you carry no longer float out in the cosmos but pulse within your breath—

That's when you know...

You've stopped searching for the stars.
And started remembering that you *are* one.

From Cosmic Echoes to Living Light

The signs were never just out there—they were always inside me.

The stars I longed for... the guidance I sought... the messages I chased...
They were planted in my own soul all along.

And in one quiet moment—when I stopped searching and simply remembered—I realized:
We're not just here to reach for the stars.
We're here to become them.

Return to the Stars—
A Soul's Remembrance

"Somewhere beyond memory, your soul remembers the stars. Not as a place to escape to—but as the light you came to embody."

There are moments on the spiritual path when something stirs so gently it could almost go unnoticed—until it doesn't. That day, it was the attic. I hadn't planned to go up there, but something pulled at me—a quiet nudge I couldn't explain. The air was thick with the scent of dust and wood, and the late afternoon sun streamed through the single window, illuminating tiny flecks dancing like stardust in the air.

Earlier in this book, I briefly mentioned a painting that resurfaced unexpectedly—one filled with dolphins and cosmic light. But what I didn't share was how profound that moment truly was. It was more than a rediscovery. It was a homecoming. And in that attic, surrounded by the quiet hum of memory, I felt the invitation rising—not just toward the painting, but toward the part of me that created it.

I moved boxes aside, one by one, not even sure what I was looking for. Then my hand settled on something I hadn't seen in years—a worn pad of watercolor paper, the kind I used back when painting was more meditation than hobby. The pages were yellowed at the edges, curled slightly as if time had breathed gently on each one.

When I picked it up, something slipped from between the pages.
It fluttered to the floor in slow motion, landing face-up with an almost sacred stillness.

A painting. Mine.

A pod of dolphins swam through a cosmic sea, surrounded by stardust and waves of indigo light. My breath caught. I knelt down and touched the edges like I might wake it up—or wake up something in me. I remembered sitting cross-legged on the floor of our old home, paints scattered around me, feeling compelled—almost guided—to capture this image I didn't understand. Why dolphins? Why the stars? Why the vastness of space calling through water?

At the time, I didn't have answers. Only the pull to create. So I painted, then tucked it between the blank pages of the pad—like a secret waiting for the right moment to be found.

And now, years later, that moment had come.

The dolphins weren't just symbols. They were messengers. Gatekeepers. Reminders.

That painting wasn't simply an expression of imagination.

It was a soul-stamped message I left for my future self.

A breadcrumb on the path of remembrance.

And I had finally come back to the part of me that knew how to follow it.

Messengers of the Deep— The Dolphin Connection

The moment I saw the painting again, something deep inside me stirred— older than this lifetime, beyond language. The dolphins weren't just an artistic choice. They were a frequency. A memory. A message from a part of myself that knew long before my human mind could understand.

I've always felt drawn to dolphins, long before I ever read a single spiritual book or heard anyone talk about starseeds. I didn't know why their presence calmed me. Or why, when I watched them move through water, something inside me softened. But I now believe it's because dolphins hold the vibration of home.

Many spiritual traditions and galactic teachings describe dolphins as interdimensional beings—sentient carriers of wisdom, sound, and frequency. Some say they are emissaries of Sirius, tasked with anchoring higher consciousness into Earth's waters. Others suggest they are memory-keepers, using echolocation not just to navigate their world but to activate dormant codes in ours.

Whether myth or metaphysical truth, I know this: their presence has always felt like a language I somehow remembered, but never fully spoke.

And maybe I wasn't meant to speak it. Maybe I was meant to feel it. To paint it. To live it.

Looking at those dolphins again, I didn't just see animals—I saw *movement across dimensions*. I saw the graceful translation of energy into form. I saw love, joy, unity. And I saw a part of myself that had been trying to surface for years.

Sirius—the star system so many ancient cultures revered—has always felt close to me, even before I consciously understood why. The Egyptians aligned the pyramids with Sirius. The Dogon tribe of Mali had complex astronomical knowledge of Sirius B long before telescopes existed. For them, Sirius wasn't just a star—it was a point of origin.

And yet, what came to me wasn't the well-known Sirius A or B. What whispered to my soul was something less discussed. A different frequency altogether.

Sirius C.

Not a scientific designation, but a spiritual one. A vibration beyond data. A frequency I didn't learn—I *remembered*.

It came through not in visions, but in subtle shifts. In sensations. In knowing without knowing how I knew. It came in the stillness. In the space between thoughts. It came through art, sound, and water.

And it came most clearly the day I held that painting again.

That was the day it began.

The remembrance. The return. The quiet unraveling of everything I thought I had forgotten.

Now, that painting hangs in my office, a gentle witness to this next chapter. I see it every day. And every time I do, it reminds me: I didn't imagine this. I remembered it.

Sirius C is not something I can define neatly. It is something I *am*. I believe it carries the codes of gentle power, of unity through resonance, of remembrance through joy. Not flashy, not loud—just pure. Deep. Expansive.

Like the dolphins.

Like home.

The Cost of Hiding: When Truth Feels Too "Woo"

For a long time, I kept parts of my truth tucked away, just like that painting in the attic.

Not because I didn't believe in them—but because I didn't think others would. I had already spent years learning to use my voice, to overcome childhood wounds and fear of visibility. But speaking about galactic origins? Frequencies from Sirius? That was a different kind of vulnerable. A deeper layer of being seen.

There's something uniquely terrifying about stepping forward with the part of you that doesn't come with credentials or a how-to guide. The part that's felt, not proven. The part that moves through the unseen.

I'd been called "woo-woo" more than once. "Out there." Even a "wack-job" by people who didn't understand why I believed what I did. So, I kept the more cosmic parts of my experience private. I walked between worlds—grounded in spiritual business and deep soul work—but still cautious about how far into the stars I let myself speak.

And then came a conversation that cracked something open inside me.

It was with JJ, of *Activations with JJ*, whose frequency-based work touches realms most don't even have language for yet. During our time together, she mentioned something unexpected—something I had never heard before:

The moment she said "Sirius C.", I felt it ripple through me like a tuning fork had struck the center of my soul...

I didn't need a history or explanation. I didn't even ask for one. I just knew.

It bypassed logic and landed directly in my heart. It was like being called by your true name after lifetimes of not remembering. And in that moment, I realized I wasn't making this up. I wasn't pretending. I was *remembering*.

That conversation became a pivot point. I could no longer deny the truth of who I am just because others might not understand. My path was never meant to make sense to everyone—it was meant to activate the ones who feel it too.

Since then, I've stopped trying to translate my truth into something more palatable. I've started trusting that the right souls will hear me in the language of light—whether I speak it aloud or not.

And the ones who don't?

They were never meant to understand.

The Ones Who Remember— Starseeds on Earth

We didn't come here to blend in.

We came to remember.

The word *starseed* can feel overused these days, reduced to a label or aesthetic. But beneath the surface, beyond trends or TikTok filters, the essence of being a starseed isn't about identity—it's about mission. It's about frequency. It's about *home*.

Not the kind you drive to.
The kind that lives in your cells.
The kind that echoes when you hear a truth that no one else around you can validate, but you *know it anyway*.

To be a starseed is to hold a memory that defies explanation. A knowing that Earth is not your first sky. A pull toward the stars that isn't escapism, but *purpose*. Because we didn't come here to flee this world. We came to help anchor a new one.

That doesn't mean it's been easy. For many of us, the human experience has felt disorienting, heavy, or even lonely at times. We've tried to make sense of our sensitivity, our dreams, our inability to fully conform. But what if those very things are the keys? What if that ache for something more isn't a wound—but a whisper? A map written in memory, waiting to be followed.

What if you were never meant to forget?

And here's the extraordinary thing—we're not the only ones remembering.

Children today are arriving already awake. They carry frequencies we once had to fight to access. They speak of other planets, past lives, energy fields, and invisible friends with a clarity that can't be dismissed as imagination. They *know.* And they aren't afraid to say so—until someone teaches them to be.

As adults, parents, and mentors, our role is no longer just to teach. It's to listen. To honor. To create space for what they already remember, instead of shutting it down because we don't yet understand it. These children are not here to be molded. They are here to remind us.

To remind us that remembrance is not something we earn—it's something we *allow.*

So many of us are waking up. Not all at once—but in waves. We're finding one another, sometimes through books like this, or in conversations that start with: "This might sound crazy, but..."

It's not crazy. It's encoded. It's remembered. And it's time.

You are not here by accident. If you've always felt different, if you've sensed things others couldn't name, if you've longed for "home" without knowing where that is—you are not alone.

You are one of the ones who remember.

You came with a frequency. A mission. A gift.

And no matter how quiet it's been, no matter how long it's slept beneath layers of survival, it's still there—intact. Untouched. Ready.

Because Earth doesn't need more noise.

It needs remembrance.
It needs grounded light.

It needs *you*.

And it needs you to **hold the light steady** for the ones who are just arriving—with their eyes wide open and their hearts still intact.

The Seeding—A Soul's Ancient Assignment

There's a reason this remembrance doesn't feel new. Because it isn't.

I've come to understand that this isn't just my first lifetime awakening to something galactic. It's a *return* to something I've known long before this body. And the confirmations didn't arrive all at once—they came gently, over time, like whispers returning through the people drawn into my life.

The first came from Aurora, my trusted mentor and friend. I first discovered her when she spoke on *Beyond the Ordinary* with John Burgos. Something about her energy resonated so deeply that I purchased a session, and that's how we first met, face to face on Zoom. During that first conversation, she looked at me—not with curiosity, but with recognition and said something I've never forgotten: *"You were part of the group that seeded Earth."*

At the time, I didn't know how to respond. I couldn't explain why her words moved through me like an ancient bell ringing in a deep chamber. I just knew something had shifted. It wasn't that I believed her blindly. It was that, hearing it, I *remembered*.

Three years later, Aurora brought it up again. As if to anchor it more fully. As if to say: *Don't forget. This is part of your soul's origin.*

And then came another voice—Jessa, a newer connection whose grounded presence felt immediately trustworthy. We were exploring my Galactic Chart together in a Telegram chat, so yes, I expected the conversation to be galactic in nature. But what she shared still caught me off guard: she told me I had been part of a smaller Andromedan collective, one specifically tasked with embedding codes directly into Earth's first planned civilizations.

Her words aligned with what Aurora had shared years earlier—but offered a layer of clarity that unlocked something deeper.

From their insights—and the inner resonance that followed—I came to understand that my light body existed before Lemuria had fully formed, before light began to separate into incarnations of its own. When that separation began, a part of me—a soul aspect—incarnated into Lemuria.

That was my first Earth lifetime.

And even now, lifetimes later, I can feel the thread hasn't been broken. I still carry the codes. I still walk with the mission.

This isn't mythology for me. This is memory.
It's not fantasy. It's *familiar*.

So when I held that painting again...
When JJ named *Sirius C*...
When the stars began whispering in a language I didn't need to translate...

I didn't need proof.
I needed to trust what I'd already lived.

And maybe, just maybe—you have too.

The Myth of "Spiritual Enough"

For a long time, I didn't think I was truly "spiritual enough."

Not because I lacked belief—but because I didn't experience things the way others seemed to. I'd hear people talk about past lives in vivid detail, channeling messages from guides while in deep trance, or recalling their

Akashic records like reading a well-worn book. And I'd think to myself, *Why can't I do that?*

I never felt like I channeled—at least not in the way I thought you were supposed to. In my mind, channeling meant going into a meditative or trance-like state, opening a specific portal, and bringing through a message with a clear "this guide said this" kind of delivery. That wasn't my experience.

What I've come to realize is that channeling isn't always dramatic. It doesn't always come with visions or voices. Sometimes, it's quiet. Subtle. A sentence that drops in while you're brushing your teeth. A knowing that floods your body without explanation. A frequency that wraps around your heart when you're standing in nature and suddenly understand something you've never read in a book.

That, too, is channeling.

But I didn't know that then. So I questioned myself. I wondered if I was missing something—or worse, pretending. I compared my path to others who seemed to have access to things I couldn't quite reach.

It took time for me to realize that my access wasn't broken. It was just different.

It was embodied. Felt. Lived.
It didn't need to be translated—it was already integrated.

You don't have to channel the way someone else does to be in communion with spirit.

You don't need to speak light language, recall every lifetime, or know the name of your guide to be aligned with your highest self.

What matters is that you listen. That you trust. That you recognize your way is sacred, too.

The moment I stopped trying to channel *like* others, I finally realized...

I had been channeling *all along*.

The Portal Revisited—
What the Painting Meant All Along

When I first found the painting again, it felt like a gentle shock—like stumbling upon a love letter I'd written to myself and forgotten. But now, after everything I've remembered, I see it differently.

It wasn't just art.
It was an activation.
A message planted in time, waiting for the moment I'd be ready to receive it.

The dolphins weren't chosen at random. They were guides. Keepers. Symbols of something I didn't have language for yet. They swam not just through water, but through frequency—through memory. And the space around them, once just "background," now felt unmistakably like the cosmos.

The stardust, the movement, the feeling of floating between worlds—I hadn't painted it with conscious intention. But my soul had. My soul remembered.

It's funny how we create things without understanding their significance until much later. That painting was never meant to be framed. It was meant to be found. To call me back when I was ready to step into everything I once thought was "too much" or "too far out."

In many ways, the painting marked the beginning of this entire journey. Even hidden away, its energy continued to work in the background. It held a vibration my mind wasn't ready to interpret—but my heart never forgot.

And now, I wonder how many of us have something like that.

A journal entry. A childhood sketch. A recurring dream. A phrase that echoes inside us for years without explanation.

Maybe we all leave breadcrumbs for ourselves.
Maybe we all carry portals.

Mine just happened to be tucked inside a dusty pad of watercolor paper, waiting for me in the attic.

But yours could be anywhere.

Anchoring the Light—
A Remembrance for the Road Ahead

We are the bridge between worlds—between what has been and what is becoming.

Between the stories we've lived and the ones still waiting to be remembered.

This journey, for me, hasn't been about escaping into the stars. It's been about bringing the light of those stars back here—into this body, this moment, this life.

We didn't come here to bypass our humanness. We came to embody divinity *through* it.

To walk with both grief and grace.
To remember who we are—without forgetting why we're here.

To carry ancient wisdom in one hand, and the beautiful mess of modern life in the other—and know that both are sacred.

That is the real work of remembrance.

It's not about proving your galactic lineage or earning some kind of spiritual badge. It's about softening into your soul's frequency and letting it ripple through the way you speak, the way you love, the way you lead.

It's about choosing to live as a light being in a world that often forgets the light.

And that choice? That's what changes everything.

So if you've been waiting for a sign... for permission... for the right moment to step fully into who you are, let this be it.

Because the painting has been found.
The memories have returned.
The frequencies are rising.
And you—beautiful, eternal soul—you are waking up.

Not to escape.

But to arrive.
To anchor.
To lead with light.
To live with light.

To *be* the light.

And most of all...

To trust the voice within.

Because the whispers you've heard along the way?

The nudges, the knowings, the truths too soft to be spoken out loud?

They weren't just echoes from beyond.

They were *your* voice.
Calling you home.

The final word has been written.

But your voice?

It's just beginning to rise.

The Space Between

"Some journeys don't end. They ripple outward—living in the hearts they've touched."

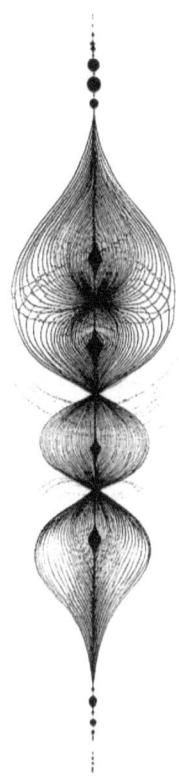

Acknowledgments

There are so many beautiful souls—both seen and unseen—who have guided my path to this moment.

To John Burgos, Producer and Host of *Beyond the Ordinary Show*, and to Emilio Ortiz, Creator and Host of *Just Tap In*—thank you for creating spaces where truth seekers can discover new perspectives and awakenings. Your work planted seeds that took root in my life in ways too profound to measure.

To Dr. Joe Dispenza, whose teachings helped me understand the power of energy and intention on a deeper level—thank you for showing us the bridge between science and spirit.

To Aurora Luna Star, mentor, friend, and luminous guide—your presence has been a blessing beyond words, illuminating my journey with unwavering love, wisdom, and grace.

And to JJ Brighton—it was a single conversation with you that sparked the vision for *The Sacred Success Blueprint*. Your light ignited a new path of creation, and I am forever grateful.

To my beloved team of light—my unseen companions and guides—you have whispered when I was willing to listen, nudged me when I needed courage, and wrapped me in love when I forgot who I was. Thank you for walking beside me always. Your presence has been the quiet compass guiding me home.

And to you, the reader—thank you for stepping onto this path of remembrance.

Your willingness to explore, to question, and to open your heart is part of a much greater unfolding.

May your own journey be filled with light, grace, and the deep, abiding knowing that you are never walking alone.

Afterword–A New Dawn Rising

As we bring this journey to a close, I want to leave you with one simple truth:

You are the light you have been waiting for.

The world around us is undergoing a profound shift.

What may appear as chaos is actually a sacred unraveling—a clearing away of fear-based structures that no longer serve humanity's highest good.

We are witnessing the birth of a new Earth—a return to unity consciousness, where love, sovereignty, and soul remembrance are the guiding lights; where, beyond all our differences, we are connected by something eternal: love.

Your journey matters.

Your voice matters.

Your light matters.

If this book stirred something within you, it was not by accident. Your soul is calling you home—to your own truth, to your own divine nature, to the role you came here to play in this beautiful unfolding.

As for me, my journey continues.

I move forward with a heart open to the unknown, guided by the whisperings of Spirit, the harmonies of Light Language, and the sacred call to embody all that I came here to be.

Wherever you go from here, trust your journey.

Even when the road feels uncertain, know that you are being led by something greater than you can see. You are never alone.

Every choice you make to honor your heart helps illuminate the way for others—and together, we are creating a new world.

This is not the end.
It is a beginning.
A homecoming to the light within you that has been there all along.

And from this place of remembrance, may you walk forward not as someone seeking the light—
but as someone living it.

Let your life become the transmission.
Let your presence become the prayer.
You don't need to have it all figured out—you only need to keep showing up, aligned and willing.
Because every step you take in truth sends ripples into the collective field.

The path ahead is yours to shape.
And the cosmos within you is ready to rise.

With infinite gratitude and love,

Cheryl

The Ripple We Become

Thank you for walking this sacred journey with me.

If something stirred within you as you turned these pages, know it was not by accident. A deeper remembering is awakening—and this is only the beginning.

To support your continued unfolding, I've created something special for readers of *Voices*:

Reset and Rise —*A Sacred Bundle to Reconnect, Realign, and Rise Higher*

This free gift includes guided meditations, a soul-aligned mini-course, and printable tools to help you:

- Release stress and emotional clutter
- Reconnect with your center and authentic self
- Step into aligned momentum—grounded, clear, and inspired

Inside the bundle, you'll receive:

The Sacred Reset Meditation Collection—10 deeply nourishing audio meditations

Success Within Mini-Course—Realign with your purpose through intuitive daily rituals

Bonus Practices—Stress release, morning clarity, and evening centering meditations

Printable Tools—A companion workbook, habit tracker, journal templates, and more

Claim your free Reset and Rise Bundle here:

awakenspiritualpath.com/reset-rise-gift

This is your invitation to pause, realign, and rise into the intuitive, empowered being you came here to be.

Bonus Gift

Because this journey doesn't end here—it ripples outward—I'll also be gifting you something soon:

A *Soul Reflection Journal*—a printable PDF with channeled prompts to deepen your integration and activate what this book stirred within you.

This guided tool will invite you to:

- Reflect on what you've remembered
- Embody the shifts unfolding within
- Stay anchored in your light as you rise

You'll receive it as a gift from my heart—a companion to revisit whenever you need to reconnect with your truth.

We don't have to walk this path alone.
We are part of something greater.
A shared ripple of awakening, rising, and remembering.

Let's become the light, together.

To your unfolding,

Cheryl T Campbell

Cheryl T Campbell
awakenspiritualpath.com

www.ingramcontent.com/pod-product-compliance
Lightning Source LLC
Chambersburg PA
CBHW021716120626
46545CB00004B/1591